W. SOMERSET MAUGHAM

Literature and Life: British Writers

Selected list of titles in the series:

Complete list of titles in the series available from publisher on request.

W. SOMERSET MAUGHAM

Archie K. Loss

UNGAR • NEW YORK

1987

The Ungar Publishing Company
370 Lexington Avenue, New York, NY 10017

Printed in the United States of America

Library of Congress Cataloging-in-Publication Data

Loss, Archie K. (Archie Krug)
  W. Somerset Maugham.

  (Literature and life. British writers)
  Bibliography: p.
  Includes index.
  1. Maugham, W. Somerset (William Somerset),
1874–1965 — Criticism and interpretation.
I. Title. II. Series.
PR6025.A86Z68   1987   823'.912   87-10901
ISBN 0-8044-2544-2

Acknowledgment is made for permission to quote excerpts from the following works: *The Circle*, copyright 1921 by W. Somerset Maugham; *The Constant Wife*, copyright 1926 by W. Somerset Maugham; *Our Betters*, copyright 1921 by W. Somerset Maugham; *The Sacred Flame*, copyright 1928 by W. Somerset Maugham. Reprinted by permission of Doubleday and Company, Inc. and the Executors of the Estate of W. Somerset Maugham.

Again, for SUZANNE

Contents

Chronology

1874   William Somerset Maugham is born in Paris on January 25, the fourth son of Edith and Robert Ormond Maugham, a lawyer who handled the affairs of the British Embassy.

1882   Maugham's mother dies of consumption and complications of childbirth on January 31, six days after his eighth birthday.

1884   Maugham's father dies of cancer on June 24, leaving an estate of less than five thousand pounds for his five sons; Maugham goes to England to live with his Uncle Henry, vicar of the parish of All Saints in Whitstable, Kent, and his German-born wife Sophie.

1885   Maugham enters King's School in Canterbury.

1889   He leaves King's School after recuperating from a bout of pleurisy in Hyères, in the south of France.

1890   He goes to Germany to attend the University of Heidelberg and there meets English aesthete Ellingham Brooks, with whom he has his first homosexual affair; he is also exposed to Arthur Schopenhauer and Henrik Ibsen, two major early influences.

1892   He returns to England and tries his hand at accounting, which he gives up after one month;

he finally elects to study medicine at St. Thomas's Hospital in London, where he gains much experience of value to his early writing.

1897   *Liza of Lambeth*, his first novel, is published to favorable reviews; he also passes his medical exams, though he has already decided that he will not practice.

1898   He publishes his second novel, *The Making of a Saint*, the first of a series of books of at best moderate success; he spends this year and part of the next in Spain.

1899   He completes "The Artistic Temperament of Stephen Carey," an early version of *Of Human Bondage*, but it is turned down by his publisher.

1903   His first play to be produced in England, *A Man of Honour*, opens on February 22 at the Stage Society and runs for only two performances.

1904   He meets Gerald Kelly, the painter, for the first time; Kelly was to paint Maugham many times and become a lifelong friend.

1905   He moves to Paris, where he becomes acquainted with Arnold Bennett.

1906   He travels to Greece and Egypt—the first of his longer journeys—and then returns to London to live; in April he meets Ethelwyn Sylvia Jones ("Sue"), daughter of playwright Henry Arthur Jones and the model for Rosie Driffield in *Cakes and Ale*; they have an affair.

1907   On October 26 *Lady Frederick* opens on the
          London stage, becoming Maugham's first great
          theatrical success.

1908   By the middle of this year, Maugham has four
          plays running at the same time in the West End.

1910   As one of the most successful playwrights in the
          history of the British theater, Maugham takes his
          first trip to the United States; he also meets Hugh
          Walpole, the original of Alroy Kear in *Cakes and
          Ale*, and Syrie Barnardo Wellcome, with whom
          he eventually has an affair that leads to marriage.

1913   His marriage proposal to Sue Jones is rejected.

1914   After the outbreak of World War I, Maugham
          joins an ambulance unit in France as a Red Cross
          volunteer; he meets Gerald Haxton, who becomes
          his lifelong secretary, companion, and lover.

1915   *Of Human Bondage* appears on both sides of the
          Atlantic to an initially weak reception; a sympa-
          thetic review by Theodore Dreiser in the *New
          Republic* brings the book the attention it deserves;
          in the same year Syrie gives birth to a child,
          named Liza, she has had by Maugham;
          Maugham meanwhile joins the British Intelligence
          Service, an experience that leads to the adventures
          recounted later in *Ashenden*.

1916   He begins writing for the theater again, with the
          comedy *Caroline*; he sets out on his first journey
          to the East, from which he is to derive so much
          material for his fiction, with Gerald Haxton as

his companion; in San Francisco, on his way, he meets wealthy broker Bert Alanson, who is to prove important to his future fortune.

1917   On May 26, he marries Syrie, now finally divorced, in Jersey City, New Jersey; by summer he accepts an offer from the Intelligence Service to undertake a mission to Russia, now in the throes of internal conflict; the trip brings on a bout of tuberculosis that puts him in a sanatorium.

1919   In April *The Moon and Sixpence* appears in England; in its view of heterosexual relations, the book reflects the deterioration of his relationship with Syrie.

1921   *The Circle*, his finest play, opens on March 3 in London; in September his most famous short story, "Rain," appears in the collection *The Trembling of a Leaf*.

1926   He decides to buy a house on the French Riviera, to be called the Villa Mauresque, where he will live with Gerald Haxton; he and Syrie formalize their arrangement of living apart.

1927   Syrie decides to file for divorce, an action completed two years later.

1928   *Ashenden* appears.

1930   *Cakes and Ale* appears to great success, partly because it is viewed as a roman à clef; Maugham reaches the height of his popularity as an author during this decade.

1933   His last play, *Sheppey*, opens in September in London.

1934   He renews his acquaintance with Eddie Marsh, who is to be important to the editing of his manuscripts from now until Marsh's death in 1953.

1937   In December he leaves for India to gather material for *The Razor's Edge*.

1938   *The Summing Up* appears.

1940–41   He and Gerald leave France when the Nazis invade; Maugham ultimately settles alone in a house built for him in South Carolina by his American publisher, Nelson Doubleday; he travels throughout the United States giving speeches on behalf of the British war effort.

1944   *The Razor's Edge*, his last important novel, appears; in the same year Maugham is devastated by the death of Gerald.

1945   Alan Searle becomes Maugham's new secretary-companion.

1946   He and Alan return to France and the Villa Mauresque, where they are to reside for Maugham's remaining years.

1948   He publishes his last novel, *Catalina*.

1955   Syrie dies; in the years following, Maugham's
            relationship with his daughter Liza deteriorates,
            along with his mental health.

1965   Maugham dies on December 15.

W. SOMERSET MAUGHAM

1

Disorder and Early Sorrow: Maugham's Life and Times

The most important events in the life of William Somerset Maugham were those over which he had no control. Like one of the characters in his fiction or drama Maugham was dealt an imperfect hand. Certain facts determined the course of his life as a child and as an adult—the death of his mother when he was barely eight years old; the death of his father two years later; his adoption by a childless uncle and aunt; his stammer, which made ordinary communication difficult; and, perhaps most of all, his homosexuality. The first he could never overcome; the last he could never forget; all decisively influenced the direction of his life.[1]

Perhaps most important of all was the fact that he was born in Paris, the fourth son of an English lawyer who handled the affairs of the British Embassy. France was to become the place where he spent most of his life, as did his father and his mother, who had grown up there. One reason that he wrote so much about exiles was that, in a literal sense, he was an exile himself: an Englishman born in a foreign country whose language became the first he was to know and whose culture became fundamental to his life as an adult. Exile forms a major part of the pattern of Maugham's life. It accounts for the interest Maugham shows in exiles in his work, and also, in large measure, it explains his own peripatetic life. Maugham deliberately set out to see as much of the world as

1

he could, seeking material to write about in short stories, novels, and plays. The subject matter most associated with his name became the life of British colonials in the East—the milieu of the celebrated short story "Rain"—which he knew firsthand from his travels. His travels were also an escape from a style of life with which he could not always come to terms.

The first trip across the sea, however, was not an escape so much as a forced departure. After a happy infancy and early childhood in a family that lived comfortably, even somewhat extravagantly in France, Maugham, after the death of his mother and father, crossed the Channel to a different sort of life. The death of his mother was undoubtedly the most significant event of his childhood—the one that had the greatest effect on Maugham psychologically—and years afterward he could not write about it without conveying a strong sense of the pain it had caused him.

Maugham's Uncle Henry was vicar of the parish of All Saints in Whitstable, Kent, a seaside town that figures prominently in two of Maugham's most important novels. Life with the vicar and his German-born wife Sophie was not uncomfortable; the house, as photographs show, had great charm, at least from outside, and the town of Whitstable was in most respects a pleasant community in which to grow up. The lifestyle of a vicar in such a parish was not grand, but it was not excessively poor either. There was always food to eat and a servant to help with the cooking; there was also no question about sending young Willie off to school. Perhaps the problem at Whitstable was that the vicar and his wife were childless; Willie came into their life long past the point at which they had decided, or had let fate decide, that they would not have children. Willie's aunt cared for him, but the vicar was her primary concern.

Cut off for the time being from the culture in which he had grown up, and separated from the nurse to whom he was much attached, Willie drew into himself. He began to read copiously from his uncle's library (one of the best features of the house), developing a habit that was to last for a lifetime. Wherever Maugham traveled in his later years, he took with him a plentiful supply of books. The next step in his personal journey, however, was to go away to school.

It was only natural for his uncle to choose a school that would prepare Willie to enter the church. There was no better course for a boy with little income, yet who was of the gentlemanly class. King's School in Canterbury was affiliated with the Church of England and was popular with its clergy. Willie entered there in May of 1885; it was to be one of the most miserable experiences of his life.

In his experiences at King's, Maugham repeated so many of the events common to the school experiences of other writers of his generation and after that he seems to have followed a formula: he had a bad stammer, which other boys liked to imitate; he was extremely shy; he was not good at games; in addition, to his detriment with the masters at the school, he was an uneven student—not indifferent, certainly not unintelligent, but inconsistent. He had great trouble making friends, and when he did manage to make them, he became so possessive that he stymied the relationship before it could develop.

It is also probable that while he was at King's Maugham experienced his first homosexual urges. The English public school has always been viewed both as the place where the future leaders of England are cultivated and as a hotbed of homoeroticism. Maugham's experiences at school were probably closer to those described in Evelyn Waugh's *Decline and Fall* than to those in James Hilton's *Goodbye, Mr. Chips*. Whether he were in school or not, however, his homosexuality would undoubtedly have developed; the presence of comely adolescent boys merely precipitated what was for Maugham a natural sexual urge. However natural it was for him, it was bound to be frustrating at King's since it apparently remained, for the time being at least, unexpressed.

It is worth speculating about the sources of Maugham's homosexuality, especially since so many writers in England of his generation or shortly after seem to have shared it.[2] In Maugham's case there seems to be a direct relationship between what happened to his parents—especially the loss of his mother—and his sexual identity. It is possible in fact to argue, as Ted Morgan does in his biography, that Maugham so suffered from the death of his mother that ever afterward he sought to possess her, or be possessed by her, through his homosexual affairs. In this interpretation, Maugham's homosexuality is a revenge against his mother's death.[3] At the very least he felt highly ambivalent toward women, and the pattern of his sexual relationships in his earlier years, prior to his marriage, was to avoid complete commitment to anyone. At the time he finally made a commitment to marriage, he also became committed to a lifelong relationship with a male partner, thus intensifying the paradox of his sexuality. Whatever its causes, Maugham's homosexuality remained something he could not and would not acknowledge publicly. Even in his profligate later years, when he and his wife were divorced, and, like one of the Roman emperors, he entertained young men procured for him by his companion, he kept the curtain drawn on his private life. Understandably, questions of legality aside, he could not let the public know, but he himself seemed to have trouble accepting his sexual nature. While some of his contemporaries lived with their homosexuality very well, Maugham had to make a considerable effort. His difficulties were related in part to his tendency to regard himself as ugly and generally ill-suited to human affairs. In the terminology of modern psychology, Maugham had a perpetually low self-concept. For his entire life, despite his great success as a writer and his recognition by the world, he remained in some respects the little boy who did not feel at home at

King's School, who kept wishing that he were in the arms of his mother.

Eventually, with an assertion of the same will that was ultimately to lead him to declare that he was a writer, Maugham determined that he would not stay on at King's. Some of his independence derived from the fact that his father's bequest, meager though it was, provided for his keep, but Maugham from those early years on had a single-mindedness that was to be one of his strongest positive qualities. His uncle was not happy with Willie's decision to leave King's, but Willie had made up his mind. After recuperating from a bout of pleurisy in the south of France, he decided to go to Germany to attend the University of Heidelberg. The pattern of exile consciously asserted itself for the first time in the life of the young Maugham; he traveled in this instance to the country where his aunt Sophie was born.

His experiences at Heidelberg were valuable to Maugham in several respects, but probably the most important personal experience of the trip was his first homosexual affair with the English aesthete Ellingham Brooks, later made into the character of Hayward in *Of Human Bondage*. With this experience Maugham came out of the closet; all of the repressed longings of school days found expression, however briefly, in this affair with a dilettante who was able to perceive beauty in the work of others, but not to express it in his own. Maugham's first exposure to Schopenhauer and Ibsen perhaps had a more enduring effect, though his dislike of German life led to an aversion to that country that lasted for the rest of his life.

Back in England after the experience of Germany, Maugham, groping for some form of professional life, eventually decided on medical school, enrolling at St. Thomas's Hospital in London. His choice, however, represented another paradox in his life since he entered into medical studies knowing that he really wanted to be a writer. The study of medicine became for Maugham a form of insurance: if writing failed, medicine would always be there to provide a living. His practical side never showed itself more plainly.

In the very year that he passed his medical exams, he brought out to considerable success his first novel, *Liza of Lambeth*, thus satisfying the agreement he had made with himself. Although he was licensed to practice medicine, Maugham decided, on the strength of one modest success as a novelist, that he would practice writing instead. He approached writing in the same spirit as he would have approached a medical career: it was for him not succumbing to divine inspiration but rather a choice of profession. If he had known how difficult it would prove to establish himself firmly after his first success, perhaps he would have chosen differently. *Liza of Lambeth* drew directly upon his experiences as a medical student working with the London poor; it provided a portrait of the seamy side of Victorian life; it was thought to be extremely realistic and daring. It also proved to be a difficult work to follow. Maugham did not wish to be cast as a proletarian realist and yet, with such subject matter, he could not avoid it.

As a novelist and short-story writer he faltered in the next few years. He lacked an appropriate subject matter on which to exercise his skills, and so none of his fiction had much success. At the same time he was searching for an appropriate subject in fiction, however, he was beginning to experiment with the form with which he made his reputation—drama. In 1903 his first full-length play, *A Man of Honour*, was produced in England; this play developed a complicated situation in the manner of Sir Arthur Wing Pinero, but showed little of Maugham's talent for comedy. It was produced by the respectable but commercially weak Stage Society,[4] and after it was produced Maugham decided that if he were to write for the stage at all it should be for the largest possible audience. That decision finally bore fruit nine years later, in 1907, when *Lady Frederick* became a comedy hit; Maugham was to become one of the most successful playwrights in the history of British drama, ending his career, by his own choice, in 1933, twenty-six years later.

Maugham's career spanned two distinct periods in the history of British drama and illustrates well his adaptability as a writer. His early comedies were Edwardian and turned on the question of marriage. Although he gave these comedies his special touch, they followed formulas of the day and were written with specific performers in mind. Maugham was adroit at handling the conventions and his sense of structure was strong; the same skill at handling a tight form led later to his success as a writer of short stories. By the middle of 1908 he had four plays running at the same time in the West End, a record unbroken until the mid-1920s, when Noel Coward equaled it.

By the time World War I was over, Maugham's work began to reflect other trends. *The Circle* (1921) reflects postwar British comedy in that its focus is not on marriage but on personal fulfillment. Its main female character leaves her marriage in order to find happiness. By then Maugham had also begun to write more serious plays. He ultimately gave up writing for the theater more because he had exhausted his interest in the dramatic form, feeling constricted by its various conventions, than because he had lost his audience. Perhaps he was anticipating the inevitable snub, but Maugham turned his back on them before they turned theirs on him.

While he was developing popularity as a dramatist and beginning to accumulate the fortune that was to make him one of the wealthiest writers of all time, his personal life continued to be complicated by various attachments that were either unfulfilled or unfulfilling.

The most significant love affair in the period of his life prior to the outbreak of World War I was with the daughter of Henry Arthur Jones, the English playwright of the previous generation. Ethelwyn Sylvia Jones (known as "Sue") may have been the only woman other than his mother whom Maugham came to love completely. His relationship with Sue Jones went on for a number of years and ended with her rejection, in 1913, of his proposal of marriage. She ultimately became the model for the character of Rosie Driffield in *Cakes and Ale*.

Meanwhile, in his writing, Maugham's interest was turning back to the form with which he had started his career. Putting aside his theatrical commitments, he began to deal with a subject he had tried to treat once before, but without success: an account of the growth and development of a young man like himself, orphaned at an early age and forced to live with a childless uncle and aunt. It was a difficult subject matter for Maugham to deal with, and it took him a considerable amount of time, but the result was what is still regarded as his single finest achievement in any literary form, *Of Human Bondage*, which first appeared in 1915 to a world much preoccupied by other, larger events. In August 1914, World War I had begun.

It may seem somewhat out of character for Maugham, successful writer that he was, and afflicted as he was with a terrible shyness, to volunteer for the ambulance service in France, but the gesture illustrates an important side of his character—the side that sought respectability and public approval. There was a terrific pull at this time, felt by many different writers and artists, to become involved in the world conflict, not only in England but also in Europe and the United States. As a result, the period 1914–19 represents one of the most decisive interruptions to occur in modern times in the history of Western literature and art. Maugham showed considerable courage in the work he did. He also found the opportunity, during his year in the trenches, to meet the man with whom he was to spend most of the rest of his life, Gerald Haxton, who soon became his secretary and companion.

As this association with the gregarious Haxton was developing, Maugham — again paradoxically — was also in the midst of a heterosexual affair that was to lead him ultimately to marriage. In 1910 he first met Syrie Barnardo Wellcome, the daughter of the founder of a famous set of Victorian homes for foundlings and the unhappy wife of a man much older than herself. Something drew Maugham to Syrie — perhaps her stylishness — and eventually she became pregnant with his child. Maugham felt an obligation to her, but until she could get a divorce from Wellcome there was little he could do about it. Syrie gave birth to Maugham's daughter in 1915. Shortly afterward, Maugham set out on his first long journey to the East with Gerald Haxton as his companion.

Prior to this trip Maugham had begun his brief career with the British Intelligence Service later recounted in the book *Ashenden*. In Switzerland he found the life of a spy unexciting — not at all like the popular accounts of such activities — but this first stint led to a trip to Russia in 1917, just after his marriage to Syrie, who had finally achieved divorce from her husband. Maugham had barely entered into marriage before he began to escape from it; such was to be the pattern of his life with Syrie.

On his Russian journey he met some of the best-known figures of the Revolution of 1917, including Boris Savinkov and Alexander Kerensky, but the results of the trip from a diplomatic standpoint were inconclusive. Maugham did come away with a case of tuberculosis, which put him in a sanatorium after his return. Following his recovery, he resumed the life of a professional writer. He also attempted, with less success, to establish a life with Syrie and their daughter Liza.

Since Maugham's motives in marrying Syrie had more to do with what he considered appropriate behavior under the circumstances of her pregnancy than with real affection, it is scarcely surprising that their relationship did not work out. Maugham was not able to give of himself to Syrie, and increasingly, in the years they were married, he spent his time with Gerald. At the same time he produced some of his most popular works, including the short story "Rain," the novel *The Moon and Sixpence*, and the plays *The Circle* and *The Constant Wife*. By now Maugham had achieved a worldwide reputation as an author; he had also become a wealthy man, partly through his own close attention to the financial details of his work and partly through investments made for him by San Francisco broker Bert Alanson, whom he first met during his trip through the United States on his way to the Far East in 1916.

Given the nature of Maugham's relationship with Syrie, a separation was inevitable. It came in 1926, followed by Syrie's filing for divorce the next year. By then Syrie had begun her successful career as an interior decorator (the "white" style of the art deco period was especially associated with her), but Maugham was eventually to settle upon her a substantial annual income when their divorce became final in the year of the crash, 1929.

Maugham and Gerald had by then settled into a style of life that was to be typical for them until World War II. In 1926 Maugham had bought a rather strangely designed house on the French Riviera. He got it for a good price, had it done over, and called it the Villa Mauresque. Here, amidst his art collection, in an environment that he completely controlled, Maugham led what appeared to be an idyllic life. He wrote every day from 9:00 to 12:45, had the substantial lunch of the Mediterranean countries, napped and exercised in the afternoon, had friends in for dinner, and often finished the evening with a game of bridge or, if guests were not present, a good detective novel.

The guest list at the Villa Mauresque included well-known names from the world of literature and the arts and also many members of the peerage. The Duke and Duchess of Windsor were probably the biggest names in the last category to come there, but Maugham's acquaintance with titled persons increased with his wealth and reputation and his address in the south of France. He had come to epitomize the writer as gentleman.

Even so, life with Gerald was no idyll. Although Maugham was to remain attached to him in spite of what he did, Gerald constantly strained their relations by his drinking and bad behavior. The settled life had more appeal to Maugham than it had to Gerald, and the longer they lived at the Villa Mauresque, the more difficult Gerald became. Maugham tolerated behavior in him that he would take from no one else. In return, Gerald performed his usual social service, including the procuring of young men who struck the fancy of the Old Party, as Maugham came to be called. Theirs was essentially a parasitic relationship that did not improve as they aged.

The fall of France in 1940 ended the easy life at the Villa Mauresque, though Maugham was able to pursue it elsewhere. He had survived the Great Depression with his fortune intact, but when the Nazis swept through France in the spring of 1940 he had to flee their approach along with countless others who lived on the Riviera. The 1930s had been good for him as an author. Although he had at last given up writing for the theater, he had published numerous works of fiction, including the novel *Cakes and Ale*, one of his finest achievements in the form. He had also published a volume of reminiscences and essays that he called *The Summing Up*, the first of a number of such works he was to produce in his later years.

His life during World War II was largely provided for him by his American publisher, Nelson Doubleday. Maugham came to the United States to do a speaking tour on behalf of the British war effort, but stayed for the duration. He lived in a house built for him on Doubleday's South Carolina plantation, where he finished work on his last major novel, *The*

Razor's Edge. Other British citizens who lived in the United States during the war—for instance those in the British film colony in Hollywood—were criticized for deserting the home front in a time of crisis. Maugham had not lived on the home front for so many years that such criticism could scarcely be leveled at him. Living in the United States was merely another form of exile for the aging Maugham, part of the pattern of his life.

Gerald meanwhile became active in the war effort, living first in Washington and then settling in New York. During this time, Gerald's health, long damaged by his various excesses, went into serious decline, and in 1944, the same year in which *The Razor's Edge* appeared, he died. No death since that of his mother affected Maugham so deeply. All accounts of the event and the months after it agree that Maugham took it very badly. Despite Gerald's destructiveness, he was the person to whom Maugham had felt closest for the longest period of time in his life. His death left a vacuum never completely filled by anyone else.

The period after the war, as Maugham grew into old age, represented a time of declining artistic powers, if not of declining reputation. He took another companion, Alan Searle, who ministered to his needs in his last years. He moved back to France, almost restoring the Villa Mauresque to its prewar splendor. He grew first closer to his daughter and her family and then, toward the end, further apart, becoming involved in an absurd court case about the rights to his art collection, originally intended as Liza's inheritance. He considered adoption of Alan as his son so that the art could be his.

Maugham ended his days estranged from virtually everyone he knew, outliving even his own reason. Never entirely happy in his youth or middle age, he grew less happy with age. At the end, reduced to incoherence and near madness, Maugham's exile was complete.

Maugham's life illustrates the central hypocrisy of the

Edwardian England in which he reached his early maturity. Never able to reconcile his emotional needs with what he felt was socially acceptable, he lived a lie that affected his work. *Of Human Bondage* suffers from the omission of a frank portrayal of Maugham's homosexual experiences, and *The Moon and Sixpence* from his negative feelings toward women. The tension between public and private lives also gave rise, however, to his sense of comedy—such tension is the subject of all comedy of manners, at which he was so adept—and also to the belief, so important in his work, that human motives are essentially selfish. We are all the sum of our weaknesses as well as our strengths; if in Maugham's case the first outweighed the second, as a writer he made of each the best that he could.

2

~~~~~~

Troubled Grace:
Of Human Bondage

Of Human Bondage (1915) was Maugham's ninth novel in order of publication, though not in order of conception. As early as 1897 he had begun to write an account of his own growth and development, autobiographical but in the form of fiction. However, he failed to write it to the satisfaction of his publisher. He put the rejected manuscript aside and went on to other things, but as time passed the idea of such a work stayed with him. Although he had established himself as a highly successful dramatist as well as a novelist, he found that the subject matter haunted him: "I began once more to be obsessed by the teeming memories of my past life. They came back to me so pressingly, in my sleep, on my walks, at rehearsals, at parties, they became such a burden to me, that I made up my mind there was only one way to be free of them and that was to write them all down on paper." Maugham devoted the better part of two years to this effort. The result was what is still regarded as his finest achievement.[1]

Of Human Bondage is not typical of Maugham's output as a novelist, though it is often so regarded. For one thing, it is heavily autobiographical. Maugham's usual approach is that of the observer, the detached ironist who may comment on the characters or the action but who seldom becomes deeply involved in it. In this novel, however, the central character, Philip Carey, is clearly the author's alter ego. *Of Human Bondage* is also much longer than Maugham's other novels, which typically run to only a few hundred pages, coming closer in length and structure to the form of the novella. *Of Human Bondage* has more affinity to the great masterpieces of naturalism—to the novels of Émile Zola or Theodore Dreiser—than to the more condensed form of the novella. Finally, it is a novel that, even for 1915, is quite old-fashioned in technique. In his other best-known novels, Maugham takes leaps from one scene to another and other liberties with narrative, which, while certainly far from avant-garde, at least indicate a strong interest in the more truncated form typical of the modern novel. In *Of Human Bondage*, considerations of form are subordinate to the pressing need of the author to deal with his subject matter at whatever length and, to a degree, with whatever amount of self-revelation may result. The novel is powerful in spite of its sometimes clumsy, heavily chronological structure, not because of it. It speaks from its main character's suffering, which becomes, for many readers, a paradigm of the human condition.

On its broadest level, *Of Human Bondage* deals with the conflict between the real and the ideal, a conflict to which Philip Carey, its protagonist, constantly alludes in his thoughts and which, as the novel reaches its close, he appears to have resolved to his satisfaction.

As a boy, the loss of his mother and the rejection by his fellow students at school force Philip into a world of his own making, an imaginative world that grows largely out of his reading. His subsequent attempt to achieve a better relationship with the real world—the everyday world as well as the world of study and work—fails. In the world of emotion Philip is particularly a failure. By working his way through the tortured relationship that gives the novel its name, by coming to a better understanding of what has attracted him to Mildred the waitress, Philip is ultimately able to accept himself in a way he could not earlier in the novel. If, by the end, he is not completely free of the impulse toward self-abasement, it is at least held in check by other, healthier impulses. Whether Philip's release from his bondage is totally convincing, however, is another question.

At the very beginning of the novel, two of the most important conditions of Philip's childhood are vividly established: the death of his mother and the fact that he is crippled. When, after his mother's death, Philip is given the opportunity by his uncle to take with him something in remembrance of her, he settles for a tiny clock. For him time has stopped: no matter what the future holds, Philip will never lose the sense of abandonment that this tragic event has occasioned.

His feeling of rejection is not ameliorated by the circumstances of his adoption. His uncle William is a provincial vicar, and he and his German-born wife Louisa are childless. Although Philip has visited them, he is not intimate with them. Nonetheless, Blackstable (really Whitstable) in Kent becomes his home from this time onward. His life there is, like his aunt's, confined by his uncle's stinginess.

William Carey is the embodiment of Victorian hypocrisies against which Philip is eventually to rebel. Not so much nasty as narrow, Philip's uncle sees himself as the center of the universe; his selfishness, which grows worse as he grows older, is the ultimate sin for a clergyman. While each Sunday he preaches from the pulpit the doctrine of Christian selflessness, at home he lives an existence almost totally self-centered. This contradiction is not lost on Philip, young though he is. As a result, he is drawn even more strongly to his aunt. He senses in her a vulnerability that at times touches him and also a desire to be as kind as possible to the orphaned boy. As he follows her about her daily routine, he forms an attachment to her that, if not very close, is at least enduring.

More important to Philip's development at Blackstable than his relationship with his uncle or aunt, however, is the fact that for so much of the time he is left alone. As an only child, he was accustomed to a solitary life during his early years. As he begins life with his aunt and uncle, he is alone even more, and to fill up the hours he spends an increasing amount of time reading. The imaginative release of the *Arabian Nights* and other works that he encounters in his uncle's library helps to make up for the monotony of Sundays and the unvarying routine of each week in the vicarage. If Philip is not vastly happy at Blackstable—he in fact is not vastly happy at any time in this long novel—he is at least not totally unhappy.

Outright unhappiness comes to Philip when he must enter school. For a boy of Philip's class, school—meaning public, or boarding, school—was inevitable after a certain age. Moving away from home might be postponed by becoming a day student at a preparatory school, but eventually moving away must come. For Philip—whose legacy from his parents is slim—the choices are not many. His uncle settles on the notion that he will enter the Anglican ministry—a not unusual choice for someone of Philip's background with relatives in the clergy—and he enters the preparatory school for King's School, Tercanbury (really Canterbury). Maugham was a student at King's School, as has already been noted, and in this novel he renders the scene there in the late 1880s so accurately that his account has a certain historical value.

At Tercanbury, Philip leads a lonely, unhappy existence. Taunted from the first because of his clubfoot, labeled as a cripple who is not good at games, he takes refuge in reading, self-pity, and religion—though the last is ultimately of least importance to him. In 1887, with his entrance into King's School, Philip at least finds some intellectual challenges to engage him, though certain masters and classmates remain cruel. He forms an attachment to the new headmaster—like himself, not well accepted by many of the other masters—and, as he moves on, to a fellow student named Rose. Rose has all the personal qualities that Philip lacks, and, when he turns out to feel less devotion to Philip than Philip feels to-

ward him, Philip's hopes are dashed and he grows vastly dis-
satisfied with his life. Philip's attachment to Rose has all the
characteristics of the schoolboy crushes for which the English
public schools are celebrated, and, as in the case of so many
such crushes, Philip's feelings go unrequited.

By now he knows that the life of a clergyman will not be
for him, and, letting his studies go, he sets out to convince his
aunt and uncle that what will be best is for him to go to the
University of Heidelberg to study the German language, not
to Oxford to prepare for ordination. This decision on Philip's
part represents the first major instance in the novel of his
going against the wishes of his uncle and having his own way
in the end.

In Germany, during the following year, Philip is exposed
for the first time to a set of values markedly different from
those to which he has grown accustomed at Blackstable and
Tercanbury. Not only does he enter into a different cultural
milieu, he also gets to know some fellow students who neither
ridicule nor ignore him. Chief among these, in terms of his
influence on Philip, is the Englishman Hayward. Hayward
embodies all the ideals of the generation of the English aesthete Walter Pater, who suggested that in life one must burn
with a "hard, gemlike flame," but he never is able to translate
these ideals into aesthetic reality. He becomes for Philip a
symbol of the failure of idealism; Philip increasingly sees the
world as a dark, sordid place where one survives, if at all, by
recognizing the futility of ideals. When Philip leaves Germany, it is with the determination that now he will face the world
at last. "I want to get to London so that I can really begin," he
tells Hayward at one point. "I want to have experiences. I'm
so tired of preparing for life: I want to live it now."

One part of life for which Philip is little prepared is sex.
Morbidly shy and exceedingly prudish, he has deliberately
avoided all opportunity for sexual involvement, though in
Germany he observes such involvement in various forms.

During the late summer following his return from Germany, Philip forms his first attachment, to a Miss Wilkinson, an older woman who is staying with his aunt and uncle at Blackstable. As in so many tales of romantic attachment between younger men and older women, it is the woman, who has been a governess in Europe, who takes the initiative in the relationship, making it clear to Philip that his advances will not be rejected. For the first time, after much initial shyness, Philip has sexual intercourse with Miss Wilkinson, but the affair ends as the summer does, and Miss Wilkinson, clinging to the memory of what they have had, returns to her post on the Continent.

Philip, now determined to try the law, becomes articled to a solicitor in London. To be an articled clerk in Philip's day was the equivalent of apprenticeship in trade: a way into a profession. For a gentleman, his aunt thinks, there are only four professions—the army, the navy, the law, and the church. With the first two clearly impossible and the fourth not to Philip's liking, law is the only possibility remaining. It turns out, however, to be no more to Philip's liking than the church. His experience in London, the first city of his hope, is so dismal that he settles almost arbitrarily upon the study of art because it will take him to Paris, which he has visited as a clerk and of which he has become vastly enamored. His uncle likes this decision even less than the one that took Philip to Heidelberg—but in the end, once again, he agrees to it.

Paris in the early 1890s was the capital of the world of art, so it is scarcely surprising that Philip should feel its excitement so intensely. The impressionists had reached their zenith by the middle of the 1880s, and painting was now in a period of great experimentation and change. This ferment is felt mainly in the conversation of the company that Philip keeps, not in the work they produce. His friends include only one highly original painter—Clutton—but personal inhibitions keep Clutton from realizing his extraordinary promise.

The most influential figure that Philip meets during his time in Paris is the poet Cronshaw. Cronshaw is another idealist of the same basic cut as Hayward—that is, a poet who does not practice his art, a thinker who spends most of his time in an alcoholic stupor, watching the saucers pile up by his place in the café. Though his ideas are not very original, they exert influence upon Philip and his young friends. Cronshaw is a relativist who places the ideal of beauty above all else. He is in this respect much like Hayward, but he has been willing to sacrifice more for his ideal than Hayward ever has.

Philip realizes all too soon that he does not have sufficient talent at art to be truly excellent; he will be at best a second-rater, and the prospect of eking out a livelihood as a teacher of art does not appeal to him. Especially telling in this regard is the example of Fanny Price, who literally starves herself to death for the sake of an art for which she has no talent, as well as the example of his teacher, Foinet. It is ultimately Foinet's advice that Philip heeds: "Money is like a sixth sense without which you cannot make a complete use of the other five." Philip decides at last—after two years in Paris—that he will follow in the footsteps of his father; he will take up the study of medicine at St. Luke's in London, where his father had studied. He now has his own income—having come of age and entered into his inheritance—and feels completely on his own.

It is at this point in the novel—approximately halfway through—that the focus of the work shifts from the growth and development of Philip's younger days to his growing emotional attachment to Mildred. This relationship provides the emotional core of the entire work. It is a relationship so far beyond the ordinary as to qualify as an obsession, and, rather than growing as a result of it, Philip's life is diminished in every respect. Mildred places Philip in a state of emotional bondage that he delights to be in and that he cannot escape for many years. It is truly a state of slavery, but one in which the slave is only too willing to wear his bonds. Given the nature of the relationship and the pain and anguish it causes Philip, one may well ask what in his personality makes him vulnerable to it. What leads him into such human bondage?

Although Philip has lived in several countries and studied for several professions, he remains a shy, morbidly self-conscious person. He may adopt a philosophy of skepticism or an attitude of cynicism; he may say to himself that in his life he will follow the maxim, "Follow your inclinations with due regard to the policeman around the corner"; in fact, however, it is much closer to the truth to say that Philip has put away the outward trappings of Anglican teaching but "kept unimpaired the morality which was part and parcel of it." In chapter 53 he lays out for himself a plan of study that includes the three most important things one can know: "man's relation to the world he lives in, man's relation with the men among whom he lives, and finally man's relation to himself." By the time Philip meets Mildred, he has just barely worked out the first of these for himself; he has not resolved at all the second and third. Despite his repeated insistence on the importance of experience, Philip has in fact had only one affair with a woman—the short and thoroughly unrealistic one with Miss Wilkinson. He seems largely untouched by the basic human emotions, but they are there, just below the surface, ready to erupt. "People told him he was unemotional," he thinks early in the chapter, "but he knew that he was at the mercy of his emotions." It is unfortunate that Mildred should become the first person fully to sense this quality in Philip.

There is little in Mildred's appearance that is especially striking. When Philip sees her for the first time, he likens her to a type of beauty then fashionable in painting: "She has the small regular features, the blue eyes, and the broad low brow which the Victorian painters, Lord Leighton, Alma Tadema, and a hundred others, induced the world they lived in to accept as a type of Greek beauty. She seemed to have a great deal of hair: it was arranged with peculiar elaboration and done over the forehead in what she called an Alexandra fringe. She was very anemic. Her thin lips were pale, and her skin was delicate, of a faint green colour, without a touch of red even in the cheeks." In short, she is not very attractive, with coloring appropriate to a corpse. In addition, as Philip notes just before the passage above, she is "tall and thin, with narrow hips and the chest of a boy." More important than her appearance, however, is her attitude toward her customers. At best her manner with them might be described as perfunctory; at times it is downright rude.

It soon becomes clear that Philip, far from avoiding Mildred's rebuffs, is irresistibly drawn to her regardless of her treatment of him. He realizes that, no matter how common, vulgar, or unattractive she may be, he is in love with her, and the feeling is far from pleasurable: "He had thought of love as a rapture which seizes one so that all the world seemed springlike, he had looked forward to an ecstatic happiness; but this was not happiness; it was a hunger of the soul, it was a painful yearning, it was a bitter anguish, he had never known before."

When she shows an obvious preference for the salesman Miller, Philip tries to drop the relationship but finds that he cannot. He hates himself for loving her, but he is unable to control his feelings: "The fact remained that he was helpless. He felt just as he had felt sometimes in the hands of a bigger boy at school. He had struggled against the superior strength till his own strength was gone, and he was rendered quite powerless—he remembered the peculiar languor he had felt in his limbs, almost as though he were paralysed—so that he could not help himself at all." His sense of bondage to Mildred becomes plain: "He felt that he had been seized by some strange force that moved him against his will, contrary to his interests; and because he had a passion for freedom he hated the chains which bound him." The attraction Philip feels for Mildred is clearly masochistic: his submission to her is the emotional equivalent of the physical submission he remembers from school days to the greater strength of the bigger boy. He is helpless to resist her, and the imagery of the last passage supports his feeling of helplessness.

From the point at which Philip realizes he cannot keep himself away from Mildred until his final rejection of her, he experiences a decline in the quality of his life and, at times, in the quality of his work as well. His relationship with Norah Nesbit—who has all the qualities Mildred lacks and who, at the same time, is obviously attracted to Philip—promises to provide him with an escape from his relationship with Mildred, but in the end his desire for punishment triumphs over his desire for fulfillment. Though he and Norah have become lovers, and he has felt with her a sense of satisfaction that he has felt with no other woman, when Mildred returns to him, pregnant and deserted by Miller, Philip drops Norah and takes Mildred in. In return for his help and succor, Mildred soon enters into an affair with his best friend.

Philip has been nursed through an illness by a fellow medical student, Griffiths—an experience with the homosexual overtones of his friendship with Rose at Tercanbury. Maugham's description of Griffiths's ministrations to Philip emphasizes Griffiths's physicality and Philip's submission to it: "Philip, too weak and wretched to resist, allowed Griffiths to wash his hands and face, his feet, his chest and back. He did it with charming tenderness." Griffiths has a feminine side to which Philip clearly responds: "Though Griffiths was the same age as Philip he adopted towards him a humorous, motherly attitude. He was a thoughtful fellow, gentle and encouraging; but his greatest quality was vitality which seemed to give health to everyone with whom he came in contact. Philip was unused to the petting which most people enjoy from mothers or sisters and he was deeply touched by the feminine tenderness of this strong young man." If Philip's

feelings toward Griffiths are homoerotic, it is a homoeroticism that stays well beneath the surface of their relationship.
That relationship, like the one with Norah, is at any rate soon
destroyed by the return of Mildred.

Mildred is attracted to Griffiths's thoroughly masculine
side. Philip is soon forced to the unhappy conclusion that his
best friend wants to have an affair with Mildred, but, rather
than work against that affair or attempt to prevent it, he does
everything possible to bring it about: "He admired them both
so much that it seemed natural enough for them to admire
one another. He did not care if Griffiths absorbed Mildred's
attention . . . ; he had something of the attitude of a loving
husband, confident in his wife's affection, who looks on with
amusement while she flirts harmlessly with a stranger."

Philip's amusement soon turns to desperate jealousy,
however, when he realizes that the flirtation is not harmless.
He becomes a voyeur to their relationship, experiencing the
same emotion he recalls from the days at Tercanbury, when he
would choose a handsome boy and imagine himself in his
skin: "He would imagine that he was some boy whom he had
a particular fancy for; he would throw his soul, as it were,
into the other's body, talk with his voice and laugh with his
laugh; he would imagine himself doing all the things the other
did." Similarly, he imagines himself as Griffiths sees Mildred
and touches her: "He understood Griffiths's love well enough,
for he put himself in Griffiths's place and saw with his eyes,
touched with his hands; he was able to think himself in Griffiths's body, and he kissed her with his lips, smiled at her with
his smiling blue eyes."

Philip is surprised by the degree of emotion that Mildred
feels toward Griffiths—an outright passion she has never
shown in her relationship with him. At the same time, when
he suggests financing their affair with a trip to Oxford, Philip
feels the same sick anguish he has experienced from the beginning of his relationship with Mildred: "Now that he had

made the suggestion he was sick with anguish, and yet the torture of it gave him a strange, subtle sensation." Ironically enough, Mildred begins to feel toward Griffiths the same kind of hopeless attraction that Philip feels toward her; after the weekend at Oxford, she leaves Philip once again to pursue Griffiths, who by then wants nothing more of her.

At this point in the novel, as Philip continues his medical career as an intern, he encounters a man who is to make a permanent difference in his life. Thorpe Athelny is a journalist by profession, but he is also a poet, a sensualist, and, incongruously enough, a family man. He is influential upon Philip in the same sense as Hayward and Cronshaw, but he is an idealist of a different cut. He is an idealist with his feet on the ground and through him Philip gains yet another view of the world. Athelny also has a great and enduring enthusiasm for Spanish culture, which Philip comes to share, but he is proud of his English heritage, too. He comes from Kent (Philip's own background) and considers life in London at best unreal in comparison with the summer vacations he and his family spend there during the hop-picking season.

More important than Athelny's geographical preferences, however, is his view of heterosexual relations. To him, married life is a highly traditional, distinctly unliberated experience. Since all human relations are unequal, the best human relations, by his philosophy, are the ones that are most unequal: "You laugh, my boy," he says to Philip, "you can't imagine marrying beneath you. You want a wife who's an intellectual equal. Your head is crammed full of ideas of comradeship. Stuff and nonsense, my boy! A man doesn't want to talk politics to his wife, and what do you think I care for Betty's views upon the Differential Calculus? A man wants a wife who can cook his dinner and look after his children." Primitive as this view may sound, it has an obvious appeal to Philip after his long and painful affair with Mildred. Here, in the Athelnys' marriage, he sees an example of a heterosexual relationship in which the male is clearly in a superior position, his wife delighting to serve him. Moreover, it is a relationship, for all its material limitations, that seems to be extremely happy. Philip is entranced.

The view of heterosexual relations that Athelny proposes — conservative even for its day — is the one that comes to prevail in the novel. From the time it is first introduced (in chapter 87) it forms a countertheme to what by then has become the rule in Philip's life: that human relationships are bound to be unpleasant and full of pain. As though to underscore the contrast between this view and his newer one, Mildred appears in Philip's life again, for one last, devastating encounter. When Philip realizes that Mildred has become a prostitute, his sense of guilt, always out of proportion in his relations with her, forces him to take in her and her baby. By the time she finally leaves Philip, realizing that he is no longer emotionally committed to her, she has depleted his income and all but ruined his chances.

In the months that follow Philip's life reaches its nadir. With little money left, and that little eventually lost through an unfortunate investment, he is forced to work in a department store in order to survive. Despite his misfortune, he comes to feel that there is some pattern in life, and that the result for him will somehow be good. The operation that he undergoes to improve his foot is symbolic of what is to come. When his uncle dies, he inherits enough money to release himself from the shop where he works and reenter his chosen profession. In an episode notable for its pastoral quality, he joins his friends, the Athelnys, in their annual visit to Kent for the hop-picking, and there, in a setting remote from the ugliness of London and its sordid streets, he falls under the spell of Sally Athelny, who is in every way a contrast with Mildred, now ridden with venereal disease and doomed.

If Mildred is the whore of the city, Sally is the belle of the hop-fields, the natural woman to whom Philip is now drawn.

When Philip first sees her as he arrives for his vacation at Ferne, she is described in mythic terms: "She looked wonderful in the night lit by wood fires. She was like some rural goddess, and you thought of those fresh, strong girls whom old Herrick had praised in exquisite numbers." Sally becomes for Philip the embodiment of the earth, the eternal maternal spirit to which all men are drawn, and when they finally come together in physical embrace it is with a sense of the fulfillment of needs stretching back to the beginning of time: "He did not know what there was in the air that made his senses so strangely alert; it seemed to him that he was pure soul to enjoy the scents and the sounds and the savours of the earth. He had never felt such an exquisite capacity for beauty." They come together with a naturalness that Philip has never known before, and their union represents the triumph of Thorpe Athelny's philosophy of vitalism.

Vitalism characterizes Athelny's view of Spanish culture: "Life was passionate and manifold, and because it offered so much they [the Spanish] felt a restless yearning for something more; because they were human they were unsatisfied; and they threw this eager vitality of theirs into a vehement striving after the ineffable." This "striving after the ineffable" differs from Philip's previous view of the ideal (especially that of Hayward) by its vitality: "It was not the bloodless idealism which stepped aside from life in weakness; it was too strong; it was virile; it accepted life in all its vivacity, ugliness and beauty, squalor and heroism." It is in fact a sort of transformed realism, through which one can assert one's will and confront the chance that seems to control all human actions. Through his affair with Sally, Philip both succumbs to all that is natural in life and asserts his will against all-governing chance.

Maugham's original plan for the title of *Of Human Bondage* was to use a phrase from Isaiah and call it *Beauty from Ashes*. He found, however, that someone else had re-

cently used that title and settled instead upon a title from
Spinoza, by which the novel has come to be known. In a way,
the first choice was the better in terms of the theme, for one
thing that Philip learns — perhaps the most important thing —
is that, like the phoenix, beauty can rise from ashes. There is,
he comes to feel, some meaning to human existence, and that
meaning is the realization of the possibility of a pattern. Lik-
ening his life to the Persian carpet that Cronshaw gives him,
he muses at one point: "In the vast warp of life . . . , with the
background to his fancies that there was no meaning and that
nothing was important, a man might get a personal satisfaction in selecting the various strands that worked out the pattern. There was one pattern, the most obvious, perfect, and
beautiful, in which a man was born, grew to manhood, married, produced children, toiled for his bread, and died; but
there were others, intricate and wonderful, in which happiness did not enter and in which success was not attempted;
and in them might be discovered a more troubling grace."

These reflections come to Philip at what is perhaps his
lowest point in the novel — while he is employed as a clerk in a
department store — and before he has made a commitment to
Sally Athelny. They suggest a relativism (like Cronshaw's)
that is contradicted somewhat by the later decision to marry
her. "Whatever happened to him now," Philip concludes,
"would be more motive to add to the complexity of the pattern, and when the end approached he would rejoice in its
completion. It would be a work of art, and it would be none
the less beautiful because he alone knew of its existence, and
with his death it would at once cease to be."

When Philip decides to marry Sally, he is deciding to
fulfill the pattern of life in that way and not in another. He is
in effect reducing the complexity of the pattern to achieve a
less-troubling grace. One might also argue that Philip's decision to marry Sally provides a romantic ending to an otherwise unromantic novel. It provides a feeling of satisfaction for

the sake of the reader more than for Philip. From a thematic standpoint, the novel might end on a less decisive note, without resolving entirely the matter of Philip's future. This argument would see the final chapters in Kent and Philip's growing involvement with Sally as a contrivance on the part of Maugham, a way of providing a resolution to a situation that is essentially unresolvable and a final bow to the hopes of readers that every story will somehow end happily.

Indeed, as one reads the account of Philip's development into young manhood and traces his reflections on the real and the ideal in various sections of the novel, one perceives a degree of cynicism that is at variance with the more romantic tone and feeling of the final chapters. At the same time, however, one can sense Philip's desire to respond to the feeling for life projected by Athelny. The life force that permeates the final chapters of the book derives as much from Athelny as it does from Sally. Nonetheless, many readers are left with a feeling that the ending falsifies Philip's experiences, and therefore affects the thematic integrity of the novel.

If one looks at the sequence of events in *Of Human Bondage* in the light of Maugham's biography, perhaps the ending of the novel makes more sense, though it may not be any more justifiable thematically or aesthetically. In his preface to the novel, Maugham writes, "*Of Human Bondage* is not an autobiography, but an autobiographical novel; fact and fiction are inextricably mingled; the emotions are my own, but not all the incidents are related as they happened, and some of them are transferred to my hero not from my own life but from that of persons with whom I was intimate." What Maugham has done, at least in part, is to transfer to the heterosexual realm his own dilemma as a homosexual; if one looks at Philip's development from this standpoint, perhaps one can understand better why the ending of the novel may seem false.

Philip's attraction at school to bigger, stronger boys has

been noted; by reason of his physical deformity and his personal uncertainties, he is forced to submit to them. His involvement with Rose, as later in the novel with Griffiths, is
clearly romantic, at least in sublimated form. Philip feels toward his friend all the emotions one might feel toward a
lover, and when those emotions are not returned in sufficient
quantity, Philip turns vicious. Philip's rejection of Tercanbury
after he feels Rose has rejected him supports such an interpretation of his feelings.

Up to the time he meets Mildred, all of Philip's major
relationships are masculine with the exception of his brief
affair with Miss Wilkinson and a mild infatuation in his Paris
days with Ruth Chalice, the friend of his friend Lawson. The
most important of these masculine relationships is with Hayward, who, of course, is based on Ellingham Brooks, with
whom Maugham had his first homosexual affair. Hayward
has many of the qualities of the fin-de-siècle dandy, a type to
whom Philip has had no exposure before his trip to Germany.
The older man makes a significant, if not altogether positive,
impression on him, as much for the style of his life as for his
ideas. In this, he compares with Athelny later in the book.

In the affair with Miss Wilkinson—which, after all, is
only a brief interval in Philip's young life—it is significant that
she is an older woman and also that she is more the aggressor
in the relationship than Philip is. Miss Wilkinson may end by
sending letters pleading with Philip to see her again, but at
the beginning of the affair it is she who sets the tone—and the
stage—for what is to follow. Philip, in his turn, is out to prove
to himself that he can have such an affair; he is not really in
love with the aging governess.

Most important, however, to an interpretation of Philip's
development as essentially homosexual is his relationship
with Mildred. This, after all, is clearly a heterosexual relationship, no matter how unhappy it is, and it is also clearly at
the emotional center of the novel. If Maugham has devised a

fable for his own sexual dilemma, how does this affair fit in?

Ted Morgan perhaps provides the answer when he points out in his biography that the significant thing about Mildred's description is its androgyny. She is both flat-chested and boy-ish.[2] Indeed, it does not take too much imagination to see that, in psychological terms, much of what follows, in the relationship between Philip and her, could take place between two males. There is in fact no indication at any point in their relationship that Philip and Mildred have any but the most perfunctory physical contact. Their relationship is emotional-ly one-sided, sadomasochistic, and chaste. There is little in it that could not have taken place between two young men of different upbringings and class who feel a strange emotional bond to each other. The text of the relationship between Phil-ip and Mildred is heterosexual; the subtext may well be ho-mosexual.[3]

To this point is Maugham's remark in his preface that he transferred his emotions to his hero. Mildred surely represents an amalgam of all the bad feelings that Maugham ever felt toward either sex. Philip's problem is that his emotions are distorted. He feels compelled to choose as an object for his feelings someone who rejects them—an essential part of the masochistic temperament. Time after time Mildred is given the opportunity to punish Philip by rejecting him for someone else or by abusing his hospitality to her. In this pattern, Norah Nesbitt represents the opposite case: a woman who genuinely responds to Philip, and who, therefore—emotional satisfac-tion notwithstanding—he is obliged to reject. The favored object of Philip's fancy is the one who does not respond, and the physical consummation of his affair with Mildred is achieved not by him but by Griffiths.

It is not necessary, however, to force every detail of the novel into such a pattern to see its outline. If Maugham felt difficulty in accepting his homosexuality, and it seems that he did, then one can see how Philip's emotional difficulties reflect his creator's. Maugham, ever the proper Edwardian, married in order to fulfill public expectations, not because he truly wanted to. Philip, having passed beyond the relationship with Mildred and having entered at last into his profession, must be made to marry Sally because the reader has the same expectations of him. Perhaps it is this sense of propriety — of action that fits ordinary human expectations but not Philip's character — that makes Philip's choice so disappointing to some readers. Having reached philosophically the point at which he can accept a "more troubling grace," Philip opts instead for the least troubling, and perhaps least convincing, of choices.

Just as Maugham is unwilling to mention by name the illness from which Mildred is suffering at the end, he is unwilling to give a proper name to the anguish of his alter ego. It is perhaps a measure of how successfully he manages the transference of emotions he mentions in his preface that one tends to feel the chapters that end the novel are unsatisfying and unconvincing.

Although *Of Human Bondage* has a personal element that is important to one's understanding of it, it also conforms strikingly to the characteristics of a particular genre — the young-man novel (from the German *Bildungsroman*). Such novels focus upon the growth and development of a young man who typically rebels against the principles of his parents, school, and society to go in his own direction. When these novels deal specifically with the development of an artist, they are known as *Kunstlerroman*.

It was in fact in German literature that the genre had its beginnings, with Goethe's *Wilhelm Meisters Lehrjahre* (1795–96). In Maugham's apprenticeship years as a novelist the most significant young-man novel in England was surely Samuel Butler's *The Way of All Flesh*, published first in 1903, which describes the revolt of Ernest Pontifex against Victorian hypocrisy. Some of the tone of this novel may carry over into the early chapters of *Of Human Bondage* and Philip's relationship with his uncle. George Meredith's *The Ordeal of Richard Feverel* (1859) was another important English statement in this genre, but of less importance to Maugham than *The Way of All Flesh*.[4]

Only one year after the publication *Of Human Bondage*, James Joyce published *A Portrait of the Artist as a Young Man*, another novel of the same type. It is difficult to imagine two writers more different than Maugham and Joyce, yet when they choose to write about their own experiences in growing up, the results conform to an extraordinary extent to the norms of the genre in which they are working. Though not homosexual, Stephen Dedalus, Joyce's hero, is as tormented by his sexuality as Philip by his, and he also wishes to liberate himself from a bondage that is at least partly self-imposed—a bondage, in his case, to his family, to Ireland, and to the Roman Catholic Church. As part of his growing up, Philip also liberates himself from his religion—much more easily, in fact, than from his relationship with Mildred. Stephen is weak of sight, Philip is weak of limb. Stephen wants to be an artist in words, Philip in paint. (Maugham describes Philip's approach to the practice of medicine in terms appropriate to the practice of art.[5]) Stephen's route of escape from Ireland is to Europe and, he hopes, to a career as a poet. Philip's is to his medical career and marriage. Though different in philosophical and aesthetic premises, the two novels—both part of the tradition of the *Bildungsroman*—describe a similar pattern for their heroes.[6]

Other important novels of this type to appear in England just prior to the publication of *Of Human Bondage* include E. M. Forster's *The Longest Journey* (1907), D. H. Lawrence's *Sons and Lovers* (1913), and—most celebrated of all in its day—Compton MacKenzie's *Sinister Street* (1913–14). All follow one way or another the *Bildungsroman* tradition;

all are autobiographical accounts of their authors' development, and all follow their heroes to the point where their
futures are at least reasonably clear.

An element common to nearly all such novels, in fact, is
an optimistic ending. After describing in detail the travails of
their heroes' early development, focusing typically on differences with parents and family, troubles at school, rebellion
against religion, and various impediments to social or sexual
growth, these novels usually end on a note of at least cautious
optimism. How else could an account of the development of a
character who represents some version of the author himself
be satisfying? Maugham was already into his forties when *Of
Human Bondage* was completed, so he had considerable distance from the events that he describes (compare Joyce's age,
thirty-four, at the publication of *A Portrait of the Artist*, and
Lawrence's, a mere twenty-eight, when *Sons and Lovers* appeared); when it comes to the ending of his novel, however, he
follows the genre in its tendency toward optimism, just as he
follows it in other significant respects.

The technique that Maugham uses in telling his story is
essentially naturalistic—though the naturalism is strongly
tinged by English realism of the Victorian and Edwardian
periods. The naturalist assumes that events in his characters'
lives are determined by factors largely beyond their control.
Whether they wish to or not, they are forced to behave in a
certain way under certain conditions. The individual will is
subordinate to the pressure of various historical or personal
circumstances. Zola, the great French master of naturalism,
frequently shows in his novels how people's lives are shaped
by historical and social events. In Maugham's life of Philip
Carey, it is rather personal events—such as the death of his
mother or the inheriting of money when his uncle dies—that
are the determining factors.

Time and again, during the course of Philip's long and
fruitless relationship with Mildred, Maugham stresses the

fact that Philip operates against his will. Drawn back to her after each rebuff, taking her back after each violation of the fundamental premises of human relations, Philip indeed seems will-less — aware of what he should do in his own best interests, but unable to do it. When, toward the end of the novel, he watches the doomed Mildred go into the theater on Oxford Street, it is not so much his will that tells him that he won't see her again but his awareness of her own terrible self-destructiveness. In his musings on Cronshaw's carpet, Philip thinks that the pattern in the carpet is something one may discern but not necessarily choose: "Out of the manifold events of his life, his deeds, his feelings, his thoughts, he might make a design, regular, elaborate, complicated, or beautiful; and though it might be no more than an illusion that he had the power of selection, though it might be no more than a fantastic legerdemain . . . , that did not matter: it seemed and so to him it was."[7]

Another characteristic of much naturalistic fiction is its emphasis upon grim, sordid detail. It is realism carried one step further, as if to point up the hopelessness of life. This element is particularly strong in the depiction of life among the lower classes (the milieu of Maugham's first novel, *Liza of Lambeth*) and we can see it in *Of Human Bondage* in the chapters dealing with Philip's medical practice in the poorer sections of London.

Much of the detail of the novel, however, is the sort one finds in all English novels of the realistic tradition, and particularly in works by Charles Dickens and William Makepeace Thackeray that Maugham read as a youth. The narrative freedom of the novel is also Victorian. Maugham, narrating Philip's story in the third person, moves freely from character to character, as he wills it, pausing where he chooses. One is thus treated, at various times, to the inner thoughts of Mildred and of other characters, as well as to Philip's. If Maugham never addresses the reader in the classic manner of

the Victorian novelist—the "dear reader" of which Thackeray
was so fond—he takes all of the liberties those novelists take
in their narrative technique. In this respect *Of Human Bondage* is different from the other major novels of Maugham;
their form is far more condensed, and their point of view
much more limited.

Of Human Bondage, with all its faults, is Maugham's
major statement in the form of the novel—the one against
which, perhaps to his disadvantage, all of his subsequent
statements were to be measured. Its place in English fiction of
the earlier part of this century seems to be as secure as its
place in the canon of its author's work: it is a major example
of the realistic autobiographical novel, of an essentially conservative technique and straightforward style.

3

Instruction and Delight:
The Moon and Sixpence
and *Cakes and Ale*

Philip Carey decides against pursuing a career as an artist because his talent is too small; Charles Strickland, the central character in *The Moon and Sixpence* (1919), decides that there is no other career he can endure, including that of husband and father, and gives up everything for the sake of his art. Like Edward Driffield, the novelist who is central to *Cakes and Ale* (1930), Strickland finds the conventions of middle-class English society stultifying to his ideals as an artist. Both Driffield and Strickland opt for the "more troubled grace" that Philip Carey ultimately rejects; both artists — at least in part because of this decision — achieve great eminence in their respective arts. The novels in which they figure make an interesting pair in the Maugham canon.

In subject, *The Moon and Sixpence* and *Cakes and Ale* deal with the artist and his place in society and with the sources of the artist's creativity, but they do so in contrasting ways. *The Moon and Sixpence* follows essentially a tragic curve, Charles Strickland becoming well-known only after his death, while *Cakes and Ale* is much lighter in tone. It is, in fact, one of the few novels by Maugham to qualify as comic. It succeeds, by the ancient formula that he so frequently followed in dramas and short stories, in delighting as much as it instructs. As though basking in the golden glow of the comic genre, Edward Driffield is enthroned in his old age as novelist laureate of England almost against his will.

Both novels depend for their inspiration upon the biographical details of real figures from the worlds of painting and literature. For *The Moon and Sixpence*, Maugham made use of the biography of the late nineteenth-century French master, Paul Gauguin, one of the most important figures in French painting between the time of the impressionists, who reached their peak in the 1880s, and the time of the cubists, after 1901. Maugham's own collection of French art, which was heavy with the work of the impressionists and postimpressionists, began with the acquisition, during a trip to Tahiti in 1917, of a door panel painted by Gauguin. In *The Moon and Sixpence*, Maugham transfers the tale of Gauguin's life to England, but embodies many details of Gauguin's life and personality in the character of Charles Strickland.[1]

The inspiration for Edward Driffield was the great English novelist of the late nineteenth and early twentieth centuries, Thomas Hardy. Maugham had met Hardy, but only briefly. His secondhand knowledge of Hardy's life was enough, however, to inspire certain of the details of Edward Driffield's, though Driffield is largely a fictional creation. In addition, to make the work even more a roman à clef, Maugham based the character of Alroy Kear, who is to do Driffield's biography, upon his friend, Hugh Walpole, a popular novelist. Through these associations, the novel succeeds in providing a picture of literary life in England from the latter years of Victoria's reign to the time of George V.[2]

In form, *The Moon and Sixpence* and *Cakes and Ale* are also similar. Both make use of the device of the narrator who is acquainted with the facts of the case and relates them, with varying degrees of involvement in the action, to the reader. In *The Moon and Sixpence*, the narrator, a novelist, is very much the observer who tells what he knows but never becomes too substantial as a character. In *Cakes and Ale* the narrator, also a novelist, becomes substantial enough to sleep with Rosie Driffield, Edward's wife. In both novels, the device for framing the story is neatly done and generally effective in terms of the theme. Both novels are also of a length more typical of Maugham's work in this form than the more prolix *Of Human Bondage*; they both make their point in a few hundred pages. Though the structure of *The Moon and Sixpence* is tighter than that of *Cakes and Ale*, both novels also conform to the timeworn dictum Maugham often asserted as important to his fiction: they have a clearly discernible beginning, middle, and end.

"The artist, painter, poet, or musician, by his decoration, sublime or beautiful, satisfies the aesthetic sense; but that is akin to the sexual instinct, and shares its barbarity: he lays before you also the greater gift of himself. To pursue his secret has something of the fascination of a detective story. It is a riddle which shares with the universe the merit of having no answer." Thus the narrator remarks at the beginning of the story of Charles Strickland, setting the stage for what is to follow.

The Strickland that we meet early in the novel seems by contrast, however, all too simple. If it were not for the opening chapter—which purports to summarize scholarly and biographical opinion of Strickland as it existed before the present narrative—we should miss his significance altogether, because the image we have of him is of a conventional, middle-class, turn-of-the-century Englishman whose wife is attracted intellectually to literary people.

Our approach to Strickland is in fact by way of that attraction, because the narrator is himself a novelist who becomes a guest at Mrs. Strickland's luncheon parties and, ultimately, at a dinner when Strickland is present. His first impression of her husband is that "he was just a good, dull, honest, plain man" of forty, who looks thoroughly commonplace, and of his relationship with his wife and children that it is thoroughly predictable—Mrs. Strickland's interest in the arts notwithstanding.

This first impression is soon swept aside, however, by Strickland's leaving his wife and children and moving to Paris in a decision that he describes in his parting note as "irrevocable." No one is prepared for this decision, least of all Mrs. Strickland. The narrator is persuaded by Mrs. Strickland to go to Paris as her emissary, to encourage Charles to come back. The Strickland that the reader next meets shows his real personality; for the first time one begins to understand him as he is. His hotel in Paris is neither fashionable nor luxurious. He is also very much alone. Mrs. Strickland and her brother-in-law have made the assumption that Charles must have run off with someone he was seeing in London. In fact, Charles has been seeing no one; he has run off to Paris in order to paint.

From his earliest years he has had the desire to be an artist, but not the opportunity. Now that he has reached the age of forty, he decides that he must commit himself to art or give up the possibility altogether. When the narrator suggests that he might be a failure, Strickland responds with unusual passion: "I tell you I've got to paint. I can't help myself. When a man falls into the water it doesn't matter how well he swims, well or badly: he's got to get out or else he'll drown." For leaving his wife and children he has no regrets; he now faces life entirely on his own, his first commitment to the practice of an art that he is still in the act of learning.

Strickland's involvement with Blanche Stroeve does nothing to deter him from his purpose. Her husband Dirk is a painter of the most commonplace genre scenes whose work no one, himself included, takes very seriously. Dirk Stroeve is one of Maugham's gallery of masochists—men who give up everything for the sake of their friends or their own peculiar sense of honor. In Stroeve's case, it is ultimately Blanche, whom he loves more than anyone else on earth, that he gives up to Strickland. This act is the final touch in a relationship marked from the first by generosity on the part of the Dutchman and cruelty and sarcasm on the part of Strickland. Stroeve, likened at various points in the narrative to a fawning dog or a frightened sheep, ends by losing his studio and his wife to Strickland, who cares more about the first than the second. Blanche Stroeve, in her turn, ends her life by suicide after Strickland leaves her. She has served as a means toward an end for Strickland: a model for a major painting and also a sexual outlet. When she makes personal demands on him, he drops her just as he has already dropped his wife.

All of these events are related by the unnamed narrator who has moved to Paris just as they are about to begin; about the final years of Strickland's life the narrator (and the reader) must depend upon the word of others, because after the death of Blanche Stroeve, his contact with Strickland is broken. Through a journey to Tahiti some years later, however, he puts together the details of Strickland's last years.

In Tahiti, in a society primitive by comparison with those he had known previously, Strickland at last finds some degree of happiness. He also reaches the pinnacle of his career as an artist, but, as with so much else in his life, his chef d'oeuvre is destroyed by fire after his death. This work, described in the novel as Strickland's version of the Garden of Eden, is painted as the artist, now blind, is dying from leprosy.

What is the source of Strickland's creativity? What does he hope to achieve as an artist? These questions are important to the theme of the novel. From the very beginning, the narrator emphasizes Strickland's primitive quality. He conveys the notion that Strickland is as unconventional in his life as in his art. After his first meeting with Strickland in Paris, the narra-

tor reflects, "It is not difficult to be unconventional in the eyes
of the world when your unconventionality is but the convention of your set." Strickland's unconventionality is far more
radical. For him, there is "in his soul some deep-rooted instinct of creation, which the circumstances of his life had
obscured, but which grew relentlessly, as a cancer may grow
in the living tissues, till at last it took possession of his whole
being and forced him irresistibly to action."

In his person Strickland combines those "obscure forces
of nature" that the Greeks saw in the form of satyrs and
fauns—prehistorical figures who are neither good nor evil.
The artist, in the view of this novel, is as amoral as they.
Strickland's strongest characteristic, his governing principle
as artist and man, is his desire for freedom: "He was passion-
ately striving for liberation from some power that held him.
But what the power was and what line the liberation would
take remained obscure." In fact, obscurity is Strickland's key-
note; his motives remain largely enigmatic throughout the
novel.

The character who provides the most obvious contrast
with him is Dirk Stroeve. Stroeve has "a genuine enthusiasm
for the commonplace." He paints the kind of pictures that
tourists want to buy and that other artists recognize as trash.
He is sociable, generous to a fault. Having had the choice of
becoming a painter or a carpenter, he approaches his art in
much the same way as he would have approached the building
of a fence. He is the craftsman who can draw and paint well,
but who is incapable of original thought; everything he does
is formulaic and sentimental. Indeed, these are qualities for
which Maugham's work was often criticized. In view of that
fact, it is interesting that in this novel Maugham should
present an artist like Strickland with such obvious sympathy.

Despite this sympathy, however, Maugham's portrait of
the artist as a primitive is not a complete success. If it fails, it
is because Maugham does not make Strickland a convincing

character. With English art abounding in eccentrics (Blake and Turner come immediately to mind), Maugham scarcely needed to look across the Channel for inspiration. Even so, the tale of Gauguin could have been transferred to England easily. The problem is not one of story, but of character. The reader never gets deeply enough inside the personality of Strickland to understand his motives. The technique of the novel is surely part of the problem. The reader is continually kept at a remove from the action by the device of the narrator, and, as the story reaches its final stages, when Strickland achieves his greatest success as an artist, one is at a double remove, the narrator telling of events that have been told to him. All of this is effective enough as narrative technique, but it tends to make Strickland increasingly remote at the very time his art—and personality—are presumably reaching their point of greatest clarification.

A greater fault in the development of Strickland's character is the triangle formed by Stroeve, Blanche, and Strickland. Much of the action of the middle section of the novel turns on this situation, which to the contemporary reader is bound to seem somewhat predictable, even slick. The outlines of the characters are too sharp, the differences too clearly delineated. Stroeve is too obviously the sentimental fool, Strickland too much the bastard; and Blanche Stroeve is too clearly the victim of Strickland's—and Maugham's—feelings of misogyny.

To the contemporary reader the aspect of *The Moon and Sixpence* that is bound to seem most alienating is its hostility toward women and heterosexual relations in general. Nowhere in his work does Maugham make plainer his feelings on these matters. It is as if the narrator had picked up on Thorpe Athelny's arguments in favor of male chauvinism and made them a fundamental part of his viewpoint on civilization. In the second chapter of the novel, he remarks that, with World War I, a new attitude arrived, and he soon makes clear that women are chiefly responsible for it: "We [the writers of his generation] did not think it hypocritical to draw over our vagaries the curtain of a decent silence. The spade was not invariably called a bloody shovel. Woman had not yet altogether come into her own." The narrator speaks here for Maugham, the proper Edwardian who attempted to keep a separation between his public and private lives. He also speaks for the Maugham who had married because he thought he should, and, unlike the Philip Carey of the last chapters of *Of Human Bondage*, found nothing romantic in it. Maugham's sour experience of marriage may also account for the rather caustic portrait of Mrs. Strickland.

As Strickland's wife emerges in the narrator's description of her, she is not entirely unsympathetic, but she is a thoroughly materialistic and sentimental woman who wants simply to maintain control of her husband. The narrator is shocked by her willingness to discuss her problems so openly with him: "I did not then know the besetting sin of woman, the passion to discuss her private affairs with anyone who is willing to listen." When the narrator confronts Strickland with his deeds at their meeting in Paris, he is surprised by the degree of sympathy he feels toward him. In the end it is Strickland's honesty that is most persuasive to the narrator—his sense that Strickland, selfish though he may seem, has done what he has done because he feels he must do it. His wife, on the other hand, speaks for all the forces of convention that bind the free spirit and keep it at home. She speaks for all women who—in this novel's view—shackle creativity because they do not understand it.

Strickland's attitude toward women goes beyond the patronizing attitude of the narrator, however, to the point of hostility. He feels no remorse at having left his wife and has no plans for going back to her. His children have all but grown up, and he wants no more part in the life of his family. In Paris, where he has plentiful opportunity for contact with women on a casual basis, he makes clear that he has not come there for that; he tells a prostitute to go to hell, saying, "That sort of thing makes me sick." Strickland has come to Paris to paint, and he obviously sees any contact with women as an obstacle to that goal.

No less an obstacle is Blanche Stroeve. Though she has nursed him back to health, fallen hopelessly in love with him, and left the security of her doting husband to live with him, he sees her in the end as "unimportant." "When a woman loves you," he tells the narrator after her death, "she's not satisfied until she possesses your soul. Because she's weak, she has a rage for domination, and nothing less will satisfy her. She has a small mind, and she resents the abstract which she is unable to grasp. She is occupied with material things, and she is jealous of the ideal. The soul of man wanders through the uttermost regions of the universe, and she seeks to imprison it in the circle of her account-book." In the end, Blanche has failed to give Strickland the one thing he wants most—to be let alone.

In Tahiti, in his relationship with the native girl, Ata, whom he marries, Strickland at last gets his wish. He is happy with her because she makes utterly no demands. Like the Athelnys' relationship in *Of Human Bondage*, the relationship of Strickland and Ata is totally one-sided. "She leaves me alone," he says at one point. "She cooks my food and looks after her babies. She does what I tell her. She gives me what I want from a woman." For her part, Ata remains loyal to Strickland to the end, even though she is shunned by the other natives when he contracts leprosy. Hers is the unthinking devotion of the native woman. "Women are strange little beasts," Strickland remarks. "You can treat them like dogs, you can beat them till your arm aches, and still they love you."

If the view of heterosexual relationships in *Of Human Bondage* seems somewhat outdated, Strickland's views in

The Moon and Sixpence are flatly primitive. Like the narrator—and like Maugham himself—Strickland sees women as a
threat; in the ideal relationship between man and woman, the
woman is totally subservient to the man's needs. Maugham's
sympathy for Strickland is expressed even more strongly in
Strickland's attitude toward women than in his view of art;
Strickland's attitude toward women, however, is in no sense
unconventional. In obeying some of the oldest and cruelest of
conventions, he is but a short step from the *Kinde—Kirche—
Küche* philosophy of the Nazis. Fascism stands just behind
primitivism, awaiting those who have been seduced by the
sheer emotionalism of the latter. Nothing could be further
removed from the primitivism of Gauguin.[3] "The writer is
more concerned to know than to judge," says the narrator
shortly after the death of Blanche Stroeve. "There was in my
soul a perfectly genuine horror of Strickland, and side by side
with it a cold curiosity to discover his motives." In the end, it
is less horror or curiosity that the narrator shows toward
Strickland than a kind of empathy.

This quality may account for the effectiveness of the
closing section of the novel, in spite of its primitive theme and
its rather disappointing evocation of Strickland's character.
Maugham always writes well about art, although one may
not always agree with what he has to say about it, and in *The
Moon and Sixpence* he writes convincingly about the art of
Charles Strickland. One can feel its peculiar quality nowhere
better than in the passage toward the end of the book when
the narrator gives a view of one of Strickland's last works:

> The colours were so strange that words can hardly tell what a
> troubling emotion they gave. . . . Who can tell what anguished fan-
> cy made these fruits? They belonged to a polynesian garden of the
> Hesperides. There was something strangely alive in them, as though
> they were created in a stage of the earth's dark history when things
> were not irrevocably fixed to their forms. They were extravagantly

luxurious. They were heavy with tropical odours. They seemed to possess a sombre passion of their own. It was enchanted fruits, to taste which might open the gateway to God knows what secrets of the soul and to mysterious palaces of the imagination. They were sullen with unawaited dangers, and to eat them might turn a man to beast or god. All that was healthy and natural, all that clung to happy relationships and the simple joys of simple men, shrunk from them in dismay; and yet a fearful attraction was in them, and, like the fruit on the Tree of the Knowledge of Good and Evil they were terrible with the possibilities of the Unknown.

In *Cakes and Ale* the view of art is less intense, the view of heterosexual relations and even marriage somewhat more charitable. One can account for the difference in attitude and tone in part by the passage of time—Maugham was now in his fifties—but also by the difference in genre. *Cakes and Ale* presents a comic vision of life, which—in the sections devoted to English literary life in the teens and twenties—becomes outright satire. It marks one of the best fusions of genre and tone, of form and substance, its author was to manage in the form of the novel. If it seems less brilliant or witty today than it did when it first appeared, its dulling has occurred less because of problems of theme or development of character than because the literary world it pictures now seems so remote. The novel presented to the readers of 1930 a view of a period recently past; the present scene of the novel itself now seems a period view, slightly dated, but nonetheless charming. Thus there is a picture within a picture, each more remote from our time.

Alroy Kear, a friend of the narrator, is commissioned to write the official biography of Edward Driffield. Kear's knowledge of Driffield is based chiefly on contact with him after he achieves eminence in the world of letters; the narrator—whom Maugham calls Ashenden—was acquainted with Driffield long before he achieved that eminence, and Kear seeks him out for information. Kear's queries set the machinery of recollection in motion; much of the novel is made up of Ashenden's recollections of times past.

His first group of recollections is centered in Blackstable (familiar from *Of Human Bondage*) around 1890. The background of the narrator is in fact much the same as that of Philip Carey. He has lived with his uncle, a vicar, and his aunt, who was born in Germany of good family. He attends school at Tercanbury and on holiday lives at the vicarage with his uncle and aunt. Though briefly sketched, the details are similar to those of Philip's life; what is different—in keeping with the comic nature of the story—is the tone. In *Of Human Bondage*, one is struck by the constriction of life in Blackstable, by its narrowness and lack of variety. In *Cakes and Ale*, though one recognizes how provincial it is, Blackstable basks in a golden glow of nostalgia exceptional in Maugham's work. Though the narrator says that life is better in his own day, the tone of much of his description of Blackstable in the 1890s belies his statement.

Ashenden is initially attracted to the Driffields by their differences from the mores of Blackstable. Among the people of Blackstable, who are "vain, pig-headed, and odd" and "not easy to get on with," the Driffields are free spirits who wear no "mask of respectability"; they do not cling to the class distinctions that mean so much to everyone else.

Part of their attraction is based on Edward's being a writer. Ashenden has never known a writer before, and he finds the notion of earning one's living by such a means intriguing. Another attraction is clearly Rosie Driffield, whose beauty, personality, and complete lack of pretension fascinate the boy. Repeatedly, in describing her, the narrator chooses words that suggest her openness and simplicity.

It soon becomes obvious even to Ashenden, however, that, open and simple and childlike though she may seem, Rosie Driffield is not totally honest in her relations with

Edward. Stories have long circulated about her past life. The boy sees current evidence of the truth of them as he observes her meeting with a man once reputed to be her lover, Lord George Kemp, the embodiment of so many qualities that Ashenden's aunt and uncle most despise. When the Driffields bolt from Blackstable, leaving all sorts of debts behind them, they bear out the bad opinion that Ashenden's uncle and aunt have of them. They seem to the vicar as they have always seemed, a pair of common adventurers.

The second group of recollections comes in the mid-1890s and is centered in London, where Ashenden, now twenty, like Philip Carey before him, has become a medical student at St. Luke's. He is also in private (like Maugham himself) a would-be writer, engaged in his first efforts at creative work. When he encounters the Driffields again, he finds their circle enlarged, along with Edward's reputation, to include poets, painters, critics, and literary hangers-on of various types. Ashenden becomes part of the group, spending Saturdays at the Driffields'. He soon observes the freedom of Rosie Driffield's existence—the amount of time she spends with men other than Edward—and becomes part of that group as well. Within a short period of time, Ashenden, some fifteen years Rosie's junior, becomes her lover.

This relationship—which has a romantic quality to it appropriate both to the difference in the ages of Ashenden and Rosie and to the general tone of nostalgia that permeates the flashback sections of the novel—ends with Rosie's sudden departure to America with Lord George Kemp. Edward, dashed at first, remarries, this time to a woman determined to make him a national institution, and Ashenden goes on to a literary career.

At the very end of the novel—in a kind of coda to the main action—Ashenden meets Rosie, now grown old, one last time in New York. She retains some of her earthiness, and all of her affection for her now-departed lover, George Kemp.

"He was always," Rosie says, in the last line of the novel, "such a perfect gentleman."

Like *The Moon and Sixpence*, *Cakes and Ale* deals, at least in part, with the artist and his relationship to society. For the young Edward Driffield, as for Charles Strickland, middle-class England is something he must escape in order to realize his art, though for Edward that escape means leaving the provinces to live in London. Edward does not need the mask of respectability that the people of Blackstable cherish, and when he and Rosie bolt for London, leaving their debts behind them, they are in effect thumbing their noses at Victorian values. It is Mary-Ann, the servant who brought up Ashenden, who puts what they do into its proper perspective. "They let everyone in proper," she says after a giggle. "They was as free as you like with their money and everyone thought they 'ad plenty. . . . They ran up bills in every shop in the town. I don't know 'ow people can be such fools." In their escape from the values of provincial life, Edward and Rosie have the advantage of being born outside "respectable" circles. They have little to lose. At the same time, however, it does not take Edward long to learn that his literary success depends upon acceptance by the right literary and social circles.

London is not Paris, but, for the novelist whose reputation grows with each work he publishes, it is clearly the place for Edward Driffield to be. In this respect, his attitude differs sharply from that of Charles Strickland. Strickland deliberately removes himself from all possible contact with his artistic peers; Edward Driffield moves to London primarily to become part of the right literary circles. His ultimate success is due in no small measure to his efforts in this direction, as well as those of his wife; he is not the artist in isolation. Moreover, in the end, he is willing to become very respectable indeed to achieve the status of novelist laureate he holds in his old age.

The view of literary England in the novel is not limited to Driffield's period, however. It includes also the generation of the narrator and Alroy Kear. The view of the literary artist thus includes not only the master but also his biographer, who, like Driffield, has achieved eminence largely because of his longevity.

Kear is the totally professional author whose career could serve in this respect as a model for younger writers. "I could think of no one among my contemporaries," the narrator remarks, "who had achieved so considerable a position on so little talent." It is in fact by virtue of cultivating the right people and also by virtue of patience and longevity that Alroy Kear has reached his position of eminence. His approach to the task of writing Driffield's biography is typical of his approach to writing in general. "It would be rather amusing," he tells Ashenden, "to show the man with his passion for beauty and his careless treatment of his obligations, his fine style and his personal hatred for soap and water, his idealism and his tippling in disreputable pubs; but honestly, would it pay?"

Kear prefers to take a dishonest look at his subject rather than risk offending either Driffield's widow or the public view of the late novelist. In his biography as in his other work, Kear is, in Ashenden's words, "an example of what an author can do, and to what heights he can rise, by industry, common sense, honesty, and the efficient combination of means and ends."

The narrator's comments on Kear and Driffield are equally deprecating: they damn with faint praise. In Driffield's case, as so often happens, the reputation comes after the best work is done—after he has begun to repeat himself: "His outstanding merit was not the realism that gave vigour to this work, nor the beauty that informed it, nor his graphic portrayals of seafaring men, nor his poetic descriptions of salty marshes, of storm and calm and of nestling hamlets; it was his longevity." Encased in a public persona at odds with his private self, the aged Driffield conveys only by the occasional wink or the indelicate anecdote that he remains inwardly true to himself. The literary life has become for him as much of a trap as it is for Kear, though his contribution to letters has been infinitely greater.

The exact position of Ashenden in the literary world is never made precisely clear. He is, of course, a practicing novelist and man of letters, though perhaps with less recognition from the general public and the critics than Kear. He is in a position to be acquainted with practically everyone, but yet seems intimate with no one. He describes the artistic and literary world of England as he knew it, but with a sense of being outside looking in, not inside looking out. He writes, in short, like Maugham himself, who never felt totally accepted by the literary and artistic establishment of England and whose work was typically regarded by that establishment as not quite of the first rank. (Many of the criticisms Ashenden makes of Roy Kear's work were in fact made of Maugham's.) If one considers the substance and tone of many of the literary prefaces and introductions that Maugham was to write in the decade or so following *Cakes and Ale*, it is evident how much Ashenden's comments on literature and life reflect his own. Even in 1930, at the height of his reputation as a writer, Maugham did not feel sufficiently appreciated for what he had accomplished.

All of this, of course, is something that must be inferred from what Ashenden says in *Cakes and Ale*. As a matter of fact, most of what the reader learns about Ashenden has nothing whatever to do with literature, but rather with the process of his initiation into the adult world. If *Cakes and Ale* is in part a novel about the artist and society, it is also a novel about initiation. It deals with the growing awareness of a youth brought up in a provincial town that other values exist. Ashenden, following the example of his uncle and aunt and their friends, is a snob who looks down his nose at the likes of

Lord George Kemp and cannot understand why Rosie Driffield is unashamed of having once been a barmaid. "They seemed to have no sense of things one could do and the things one simply couldn't," Ashenden reflects at one point. "It never ceased to embarrass me, the way in which they talked of incidents in their past that I should have thought they would not dream of mentioning."

In spite of the fact that he enjoys their company, he never quite gets over the fact that the Driffields are not of the same class as he is, and when they leave town with their bills unpaid he feels a sense of shame at having been associated with them. His response to the situation differs chiefly in degree, not in kind, from his uncle's; it is not the same as Mary-Ann's. "I was much more shocked than Mary-Ann," he says. "I was a very respectable youth. The reader cannot have failed to observe that I accepted the conventions of my class as if they were the laws of Nature."

It is a different set of Nature's laws that Ashenden is obeying when he becomes Rosie's lover, but their affair completes the pattern of initiation begun some years before at Blackstable. Attracted from the first by her openness and lack of conventionality, he realizes after observing her with Lord George Kemp her sensuous nature. By the time of their reacquaintance in London, he is ready to become involved himself. Rosie becomes for him, as Sally Athelny is for Philip Carey in *Of Human Bondage*, the woman whom it is natural to love: "She stood like a maiden apt for love offering herself guilelessly," he observes of her painted portrait, "because she was fulfilling the purposes of Nature, to the embraces of a lover." The romantic view of the portrait carries over into their affair.

There, in the first encounter between the two, Rosie is very much in command, the earth mother taking the young man to her bosom: he becomes "a child in her arms" and she is the mother who rocks him into the act of love. When she leaves him after their first night, she walks with "the firm tread of the country woman who likes to feel the good earth under her feet." Once again, as in *Of Human Bondage*, the positive heterosexual relationship is the one that is perfectly "natural," in which the woman gives herself to the man in keeping with ancient and unquestioned laws.

What is lacking in this description of lovemaking—indeed, in the relationship of Ashenden and Rosie as a whole—is some sense of reality. As in the case of Philip Carey and Sally, one does not get the feeling that an honest relationship has occurred, but rather that one has been contrived to suit the process of initiation begun earlier in the novel. Rosie's departure with Lord George Kemp, after the year in which she and Ashenden have their affair, is largely unprepared for; it is completely in keeping with Rosie's character, but it is an event that does not grow directly out of what precedes it in the novel. Like the affair between Ashenden and Rosie, it seems contrived, introduced merely to bring the story to an end. As a character, Rosie is more convincing before and after this moment than she is as she becomes the lover of Ashenden and the wife of Lord George. One follows the events, but they lack verisimilitude and the appropriate degree of feeling.

One problem clearly is that Maugham has written two novels, not entirely fused into one. One is the novel of initiation, in which, as in *Of Human Bondage*, the reader follows the growth and development of a young man. The other is the novel of artistic life—in this case essentially a satirical view—which is the portrait of the literary world in the novel. One novel requires a strong narrative, with many dramatic scenes; the other something closer to an essay voice, with less drama. One takes a sympathetic, even somewhat nostalgic, view of its subject; the other a less sympathetic, more acidic, view. At some point, were *Cakes and Ale* completely successful from the standpoint of form, the two would be fused; as it is, one's feeling by the end is that they do not quite come together.

The use of the first person perhaps also contributes to the lack of development in Ashenden, because, as in *The Moon and Sixpence*, in those sections of the novel where the narrator is most involved in the action he is also most transparent. Rosie is seen through him, but one tends not to see him as he learns to know her. In the chapters on literary life, on the other hand, his voice is heard clearly—he uses the essay voice that Maugham cultivated in his later years—and one knows his opinions, but it is the mature Ashenden who is speaking, not the Ashenden who is evolving as a person.

The two voices come into intentional conflict in the seduction scene between Rosie and Ashenden. Here Maugham clearly intends to create a sense of irony, interrupting the seduction for a commentary on the use of the first person in fiction. In addition to creating an element of tour de force at this point in the work, however, he is also commenting on one of the work's shortcomings. "I wish now," he writes, "that I had not started to write this book in the first-person singular. It is all very well when you can show yourself in an amiable or touching light; and nothing can be more effective than the modest heroic or pathetic humourous which in this mode is much cultivated; it is charming to write about yourself when you see on the reader's eyelash the glittering tear and on his lips the tender smile; but it is not so nice when you have to exhibit yourself as a plain damned fool." These comments suggest that, humor aside, Maugham is quite aware of the limitations of his chosen technique. In many ways that first-person narrative voice—precise, somewhat self-deprecating, ironic, a trifle distant—is the one most associated with Maugham's name. Cynical, with an inclination toward the epigrammatical, this voice is always detached from what it describes and seldom if ever expresses great compassion.

Samuel Butler undoubtedly provided some inspiration for Maugham's favorite narrative voice, with the beautifully controlled irony of Overton, his narrator in *The Way of All*

Flesh. The general importance of the first-person narrator in nineteenth-century fiction should be noted, too. Maugham used this voice quite early in his career—a number of years, in fact, before Butler's novel saw the light of day—in several stories of *Orientations*, his first volume of short fiction, published in 1899.[4]

Perhaps one reason Maugham especially cultivated the first-person narrative technique after the publication of *Of Human Bondage* was to present to the world a persona that differed markedly from the character of Philip Carey. To the extent that Maugham could be identified with Philip, his readers might continue to see him in that light. It was natural enough for Maugham to wish to cultivate a different sort of fictional personality, one more urbane, less vulnerable than the personality of Philip. The reader cannot imagine the narrator of *The Moon and Sixpence* having an affair with a waitress; Ashenden, in *Cakes and Ale*, might go so far as to have a conversation with her.

The Ashenden of *Cakes and Ale* could serve as a model for Maugham's first-person voice in other work. He shares with Philip Carey many details of background, but his name is the same as that of the character who gave his name to Maugham's book of spy adventures, based on his own experiences during World War I and published in 1928. The Ashenden of the spy stories, like his later manifestation in *Cakes and Ale*, exists in part to remind us that there is a Maugham other than the one we have met in the person of Philip in the earlier, admittedly autobiographical, *Of Human Bondage*.

Perhaps another reason for Maugham's relying more heavily on the first-person voice as he grew older is that it gave him, as a writer who was also a stammerer, an opportunity to capture his audience with the sound of his own voice. Psychologically, the stammerer wants to hold people's attention by withholding the next word;[5] in first-person narration, in fiction or essay form, Maugham can hold the attention of his listener without such a device. He can speak in his own voice — or in the voice that he has made us believe is his — without the interruption his stammer so often provided in real life. This may account for Maugham's increasing reliance in his later work upon first-person narration, and, more specifically, for his cultivation of the essay and memoir.

From the standpoint of form, *The Moon and Sixpence* is tighter than *Cakes and Ale*, beginning with a Nabokovian chapter in which the narrator goes through the existing biographical and critical opinion of Charles Strickland's work and going on as in pursuit of clues to Strickland's character. "To pursue his secret [what the artist represents]," the narrator tells us early in the first chapter, "has something of the fascination of the detective story." In developing the story of Strickland, Maugham in fact makes use of some of the devices of that popular form. In *Cakes and Ale*, he makes use of the riskier and not entirely successful device of two narrative streams that, when they come together, as they do in the seduction scene, still remain apart. At the same time, however, *Cakes and Ale*, with its faults, remains the more satisfying novel, both in terms of form and style and in terms of characters and theme.

At the end of *Cakes and Ale*, in his final meeting with Rosie, Ashenden hears from her a long story about an incident in one of Edward's novels concerning the death of a child. This incident is based upon an actual occurrence in the married life of the Driffields, but Edward, in his recounting of it, does not quite get it right. The point of Rosie's story is not that Edward's account is wrong, but rather that life and art never completely agree. In this respect, *Cakes and Ale* and *The Moon and Sixpence* share a point that their author was to develop further, in a different direction, in his last major novel, *The Razor's Edge*.

4

Innocents Abroad:
The Razor's Edge

The Razor's Edge, Maugham's last major contribution to the novel, appeared in 1944, toward the end of World War II, and was written for the most part while its author was living in the United States during that conflict. His residency on these shores was appropriate to its subject, since most of the characters in *The Razor's Edge* are Americans, but in theme and in form the novel carries on where the earlier novels left off: the character who emerges by its final chapters as most central to its theme, Larry Darrell, is in many ways an extension or amplification of the personal qualities we have already noted in Charles Strickland and Edward Driffield, and the novel in which he figures depends more heavily than either *The Moon and Sixpence* or *Cakes and Ale* upon the narrator-as-novelist as a connecting force, giving sequence and form to the narrative, which, in this case, is of greater length than that of those previous novels. *The Razor's Edge* has its own peculiar qualities, however, which give it a special place in the Maugham canon of long fiction.

One unusual aspect of the novel I have already mentioned: it deals almost exclusively with Americans. In the opening chapter of the book, the narrator—who is in fact given Maugham's name—comments on the difficulties this decision posed: "It is very difficult to know people and I don't think one can ever really know any but one's own countrymen. For men and women are not only themselves; they are also the region in which they were born, the city apartment or the farm in which they learnt to walk, the games they played as children, the old wives' tales they overheard, the food they ate, the schools they attended, the sports they followed, the poets they read, and the God they believed in." Because "you can only know them if you *are* them," it is difficult to give such characters credibility in a book. It is to Maugham's credit that he handles his American characters so well. It is true, of course, that by the time he wrote *The Razor's Edge* he had the benefit of having traveled in this country many times for many years. He also had the benefit of having many personal friends who were American. In addition, his work had an immense popularity here, reflected in the generous sales of this particular work, which became an immediate best-seller.

The Americans with whom he deals in this novel are a special sort; they are all well-educated and well-to-do, and most of them at least have leanings toward England or the Continent. Elliott Templeton, in some ways the most interesting of them all, has spent most of his life in England or in Europe, and Larry Darrell spends at least part of his life there. The Bradleys have lived all over the world in the course of the diplomatic career of the late Mr. Bradley, and Mrs. Bradley has an extensive European acquaintance. In other words, they are all fairly cosmopolitan, and much of the novel in fact does not take place in the United States, but in France and in England. Nonetheless, given the special sort of Americans they are, Maugham's characters in *The Razor's Edge* remain for the most part consistent to their nationality; however special, they are representative American types, later versions of the innocents abroad from the fiction of Mark Twain and Henry James.

A second aspect of the novel that sets it apart from those already discussed in this book is that it does not concentrate upon the lives and fates of two or three characters. Rather, it tells the story of a sizable group of characters over a long period of time, never concentrating for very long on any one character. *Of Human Bondage*, for all its length and number of minor characters, remains in memory principally the story of two: Philip and Mildred. *The Moon and Sixpence* concentrates upon three characters: Charles Strickland, Blanche Stroeve, and her husband Dirk. *Cakes and Ale* has a somewhat broader canvas, but focuses principally upon Rosie and Edward Driffield; the narrator Ashenden is an important third principal, but Alroy Kear is important only in the frame. In *The Razor's Edge* one follows the lives of eight characters over a period of approximately twenty years; five of those eight receive more emphasis than the other three, and one, Larry Darrell, comes by the end of the novel to seem most important of all. In effect, here is a chronicle novel, albeit a short one, in which the stories of the various characters are tied together by the device of the author-narrator.

In writing about Chekhov's approach to drama in *The Summing Up*, Maugham remarks on the difficulty of writing a play like *The Cherry Orchard*, which does not focus upon a few individuals, but rather upon a group.[1] In recognition of this difficulty, the narrator of *The Razor's Edge* begins with the comment, "I have never begun a novel with more misgiving. If I call it a novel it is only because I don't know what else to call it. I have little story to tell and I end neither with a death nor a marriage." Although the novel that follows this admonition has more form and substance than this statement implies, it remains a good question whether the device works or not. Before considering that question seriously, however, one needs to look at what happens in the novel itself.

The character who prompts the whole effort, and whose life stands in marked contrast with the lives of the other characters, is Larry Darrell. When he is first encountered in the novel he has just returned from World War I, in which he served as a flier. This experience contributes greatly to his decision not to become part of the materialistic society in which he lives. He rejects the offer of a good job with the Maturin Company and also rejects the notion of going to college as an undergraduate. "I don't mind if I make mistakes," he tells the narrator at one point. "It may be that in one of the blind alleys I may find something to my purpose."

Larry's goals turn out to be largely ascetic. As he goes to live in France, Germany, and elsewhere in Europe, and then later in India, it becomes clear that his is a spiritual quest—a search for the meaning of life—which he feels he must conduct at his own pace, in his own way, earning his living as he can. With each step that brings him closer to the unattainable state of spiritual perfection, he moves further away from the ties that bind him to the other characters in the novel. Toward the narrator, however, he remains to the last fairly open, recognizing in him a stance, not ascetic, yet similar to his own. The artist, like the philosopher, remains apart from others; this is perhaps the ultimate tie between Larry and the author-narrator.

Given Larry's nature, it is not strange that he should find such satisfaction in Eastern philosophy. Chapter 6 of the novel, which has the form of a long digression, gives us a detailed view of Larry's spiritual development. In it, one sees how Larry moves from the Christian experience to the Hindu, much in the manner of so many young Americans of a later generation, the 1960s.[2] For Larry, the stumbling block to Christianity is the old, unanswerable question, "If an all-good and all-powerful God created the world, why did he create evil?" Neither Larry nor the monks he lives with in Germany can answer that question, and the failure to do so leads him to proceed further with his spiritual quest. In India, through study with a guru, Larry, to the extent that he can, comes to terms with the absolute by adapting an ancient philosophy to his present needs. Setting as his goal self-per-

fection—with its concomitant ideals of self-abnegation and
sexual abstinence—he plans to return to the United States,
support himself by manual labor or by driving a taxi, and
continue his studies.

Larry is the ultimate idealist in a world filled with people
who have either lost their ideals or have adopted strictly materialistic ones. Even the narrator, sympathetic as he is to
Larry's quest, feels in the end the distance between them: "I
am of the earth, earthy; I can only admire the radiance of
such a rare creature, I cannot step into his shoes and enter
into his inmost heart as I sometimes think I can do with
persons more nearly allied to the common run of men." As
Larry melts into the common mass of Americans at the end of
the novel, one can only guess, with the narrator, what will
become of him in the future.

Isabel Bradley—whose love for Larry ends in frustra-
tion—is not able to share his ascetic ideals. She moves from
the point early in the novel at which she is willing to let Larry
go off for a few years to make up his mind about things, to
the point later at which she comes to the painful recognition
that he is forever lost to her. She knows by then that she has
no chance to realize the love she has felt for him for so long.
Given the nature of her character, such a realization is inevitable.

Born into a family of wealth and prominence, brought
up in various parts of the world as her father's diplomatic
posts dictated, Isabel is scarcely in a position to appreciate the
ascetic way of life. She has aristocratic features characteristic
of her family, a great sense of joie de vivre, and a liveliness
and intelligence that speaks more for sociability and conversational ability than for intense intellectual interests. From
the first she feels a rapport with the narrator that corresponds
to what Larry feels, though she and Maugham seem more like
personal cronies than intellectual allies; she reveals herself to
him freely, discussing her feelings about both Larry and Gray

Maturin. She loves Larry very much, but she is not willing to accommodate her standards to his. She cannot understand why he wants to live in Europe and spend all of his time reading. "We're the greatest, the most powerful people in the world," she says of her fellow countrymen. "We're going forward by leaps and bounds. We've got everything. It's your duty to take part in the development of your country." It seems inevitable that, her love for Larry notwithstanding, Isabel should become the wife of Gray Maturin, who is spiritually Larry's opposite. In the end, after the vicissitudes of the stock-market crash of 1929 and its aftermath, she, Gray, and their children settle in Dallas, where the narrator imagines them leading a charmed, decidedly upper-middle-class life. In the end, Isabel has been unable to have only one thing that she has most wanted—to marry Larry.

Gray Maturin, in contrast with Larry, is, as the narrator puts it toward the end of the book, "the quintessence of the Regular Guy." In almost every way different from Larry, he represents Isabel's philosophical choice; the pragmatic entrepreneur who feels as she does that America is the most exciting place in the world to be. Gray is the man of action, in contrast with the more contemplative Larry; he is tall and muscular, in contrast with Larry's slighter, more wiry, build; Gray is ultimately at one with the world he lives in, with all its weaknesses and faults. His only goals are to be married to Isabel, to have a family, and to make a fortune. For Gray, who is not so much anti-intellectual as nonintellectual, to be is to do; for Larry, to be is to think. Gray's type was best defined in American fiction by Sinclair Lewis, in such novels of the twenties as *Babbitt* and *Arrowsmith*. In Maugham's Gray Maturin we almost feel that one of Lewis's characters has been filtered through a different artistic consciousness.

Gray's only moment of serious weakness in the book comes after the crash and the failure of his father's business. Like his father, Gray defines himself largely in terms of that business, and, until he is able to build a similar place for himself once again, he suffers from a sense of failure and also from intense migraines that incapacitate him for days. In spite of his weaknesses and inadequacies, Gray is a character with whom we can feel some sympathy. He and Isabel — the most materialistic of the characters — represent one approach to reality in a novel that shows various approaches, some valid, some not.

Philosophical positions aside, of all the characters in *The Razor's Edge*, Elliott Templeton has the most flavor. Elliott is also the most Europeanized of the American group. Originally of the Southern aristocracy, he has lived in France and England since shortly after the turn of the century, when he arrived bearing letters of introduction to some of the best people. He is a social butterfly and a snob, but he has gotten to know everyone "worth knowing." The narrator, hard-pressed to account for Elliott's snobbishness given his equally strong intelligence and taste, ascribes it ultimately to a form of romanticism: "I can only guess that to be on terms of intimate familiarity with these gentlemen of ancient lineage, to be the faithful retainer of their ladies gave him a sensation of triumph that never palled. . . . In the company of such as these he felt that he lived in a spacious and gallant past."

It is similar feelings that prompt Elliott to convert to Roman Catholicism and to dedicate part of his considerable fortune — which weathers the crash because he has converted it to gold — to the construction of small chapels in imitation of those of the Romanesque period. Elliott is by turns foolish and wise, but he is always shrewd about money. His death scene — which becomes tied, like his whole life, to a social event — is one of the most memorable scenes of the book.

Maugham knew the type of character Elliott represents well, having encountered it many times in many places.[3] If with other characters in the novel Maugham seems to be working from literary prototypes, in Elliott's case he is dealing with a closely observed type. Missing only from the development of Elliott's character is the logical fact of his homosexuality; one must read between the lines for that, but it certainly can be felt. At no time in his fiction does Maugham openly present a homosexual character, but with Elliott he comes very close.

The other characters in *The Razor's Edge* are given briefer treatment; they are the minor figures in the canvas, though they play at times crucial roles. Especially important among these are Sophie MacDonald and Suzanne Rouvier, the only non-American character in the book to have any great significance.

Sophie and Suzanne form an interesting contrast; the one is a woman who destroys herself, the other a woman who finds a new life for herself in her mature years. In Maugham's work the women most favorably portrayed are always those, like Rosie Driffield in *Cakes and Ale*, who take a realistic view of themselves and their chances; in *The Razor's Edge* Isabel falls into this category, and so does Suzanne. Suzanne makes the best of what might have turned out a bad bargain; Sophie (partly as a result of the workings of fate) makes the worst of what might have been at least a satisfactory one. Together, their stories form a complement to the longer, more complicated one of Isabel and her involvement with Larry and Gray, though, even so, it is difficult to justify the amount of detail we are given about Suzanne, who otherwise plays little part in the book.

Maugham dealt with the themes important to *The Razor's Edge* in one of his early short stories, "The Fall of Edward Barnard," published in the same collection as the celebrated "Rain."[4] In this story, two young men are in love with the same woman, but she favors one over the other. The favorite—Edward Barnard—has moved to Tahiti as representative of an American business firm; the one not favored—Bateman

Hunter—is in business in Chicago with his father, who, like Gray Maturin's father in *The Razor's Edge*, owns an imposing home on the lake.

The object of Edward's and Hunter's affections in this story is Isabel Longstaffe, a product of Chicago who combines American aggressiveness with European refinement. This Isabel is a neoaristocrat for whom Louis XV furnishings (compare the description of the furnishings of the Bradley house in *The Razor's Edge*⁵) are an appropriate backdrop. Bateman has learned that Edward never plans to return from Tahiti to marry Isabel, and much of the story has to do with his recounting the reasons why.

Edward, it seems, has succumbed to the influence of the Tahitian environment and begun to consider his philosophical position, his attitude toward life. Like Larry Darrell, he has begun to read simply for the sake of reading, and he now rejects the whole idea of material success that took him to Tahiti in the first place. "I haven't failed," Edward tells Bateman. "I've succeeded. You can't think with what zest I look forward to life, how full it seems to me and how significant." Edward surrenders to his friend all rights to Isabel, and, at the end of the story, Bateman and Isabel look forward to their life together, with all its material success, in what they feel is the greatest country in the world.

Edward's fall is clearly fortunate, both for him and also, ironically enough, for Bateman. As in *The Razor's Edge*, this short story presents us with two ways of life, one more idealistic than the other. In "The Fall of Edward Barnard" the alternatives are less equal in their attractiveness than they are in *The Razor's Edge*. Mixed with the desire for greater self-knowledge on Edward's part is a certain euphoria that comes (as for Strickland in the later pages of *The Moon and Sixpence*) from the tropical environment, but thematically, as well as in certain of its details, this early short story represents Maugham's first run-through of the materials of his novel of more than twenty years later. It also serves to highlight some of the major themes of the novel.

In *The Razor's Edge*, Maugham never makes completely clear whether it is Larry's way that should prevail or the way of Isabel and Gray. Part of the problem is that—as with Charles Strickland in *The Moon and Sixpence*—Maugham never quite succeeds in bringing Larry Darrell to life. As a character on a philosophical quest, Larry lacks credibility. As a result, the novel in which he figures becomes to some extent a novel without a hero.

It is true that Maugham has the narrator say that the whole purpose of the novel is to tell Larry's story, and that chapter 6, with the detailed account of Larry's spiritual development, is the most important in the book. It is also true that in one of the key scenes of the novel (and also, incidentally, one of the least credible) it is Larry, the ascetic, who teaches Gray, the materialist, how to overcome the terrible pain of migraine by the application of principles of yoga that Larry has learned in India. This overly explicit example of the triumph of mind over matter is intended to illustrate the spiritual theme associated with Larry; it overstates that theme at the same time that it shows its significance to the book.

In contrast, Isabel—though she is never able to have Larry as her own—has everything else with Gray, including a good sexual life, and the narrator, who is, he says, "of the earth, earthy," is perpetually noting the gown by Molyneux, the luncheon at a certain restaurant, and the other trappings of materialistic success that are so important to Isabel's and Gray's way of life. Furthermore, when mind does triumph over matter in Gray's cure, the result is that Gray is able to earn even more money than before. This application of the principles of yoga does not seem to make much difference to the spiritual progress of the world. On the whole, viewed in terms of actions and consequences in the novel, the more materialistic characters—not only Isabel and Gray, but also

Elliott Templeton and Suzanne Rouvier (whose real significance to the book may lie in her having this quality) — fare very well, even in comparison with Larry, and the narrator at times seems strongly to share their view.

John Brophy has noted that Maugham's attitude toward his characters can be described as that of a clinician. He notes their condition, remarks on whether it is stable or growing worse, and then moves on to the next character or story.[6] Such an attitude comes across clearly in the pages of *The Razor's Edge*, where one feels that ultimately, despite gestures in the direction of Larry, the narrator does not wish to pass judgment in his favor, merely to indicate the direction his life has taken. Despite his sympathy for Larry and despite the amount of space devoted to his story, one ends by feeling that Maugham wishes to suspend his judgment and let the reader decide.

In *The Razor's Edge* Maugham dispenses with the convention of giving the narrator a fictitious name like Ashenden and calls him simply by his own name. By so doing, he deliberately encourages the reader to identify the narrator with himself. At the beginning of the novel, for instance, he mentions his own novel, *The Moon and Sixpence*, and then begins the narrative of *The Razor's Edge* in 1919, the year that novel appeared. Later references to his house on Cap Ferrat or to his frequent travels make the identification even plainer.

More important than such details of fact, however, are matters of tone and attitude, both of which encourage the reader to feel that it is Mr. Maugham himself who is speaking. The detached, sometimes cynical tone of the narrator is the one that, by the time *The Razor's Edge* was published, had come to be identified with its author by an increasingly larger reading public. If one compares it with the tone of *The Summing Up* (1938), one can see its resemblance to Maugham's best essay voice.

In one of his late essays, Maugham described the technique of narration he employs in *The Razor's Edge*: "In this variety [of first-person narration], the author tells the story himself, but he is not the hero and it is not his story that he tells. He is a character in it, and is more or less closely connected with the persons who take part in it. Like the chorus in a Greek tragedy, he reflects on the circumstances which he witnesses; he may lament, he may advise, he has no power to influence the course of events. . . . The narrator and reader are united in their common interest in the persons of the story, their characters, motives and conduct; and the narrator begets in the reader the same sort of familiarity with the creatures of his invention as he has himself."[7]

This is a style of narration that calls attention to itself and that, by its frequent intrusions, does not have the same quality of transparency as the voice of the narrator of *The Moon and Sixpence* or some of the early short stories. It is closer in effect to the narrator's voice in *Ashenden* or *Cakes and Ale*. As John Brophy puts it illuminatingly, "The dominant reality belongs to the narrator. The reader identifies himself not with any of the characters but with the audience."[8] The technique is essentially oral in nature, and it is often digressive. It is thus part of the oldest tradition of storytelling, dating back to the very beginning of prose narrative. If one flips open the pages of the *Decameron* of Boccaccio, or of the *Don Quixote* of Cervantes, one hears a similar voice moving the narrative along. That voice may not belong to a professional author, but it has the omniscience that Maugham obviously attempts to achieve. Maugham also frequently lets the author introduce another narrative by one of the characters, thus creating the classic story within a story.

What one ends up wishing in the case of *The Razor's Edge* is that the narrative the voice moves along had more substance to it. One of the chief accusations of Maugham's critics has always been that he took the easy out. Given a choice between a conventional phrase and an unconventional one, he would choose the conventional. Given the choice between an ending that would satisfy his reading public and one that might not, he would choose to satisfy the public. These are the options that a popular author who desires commercial success is likely to choose in his work, and Maugham, first and foremost, thought of literature as a profession, and of a profession as a means of earning a living. His success in the theater was largely the result of his ability to sense what the audience liked and to provide it for them. When he left the theater, he did so for the greater freedom that other forms of writing could provide, not because he had become oblivious to the tastes of the public.

The ending of *Of Human Bondage* provides a perfect instance of accommodation to the expectations of the reading audience. In *The Razor's Edge* one suspects that Maugham was looking at the movie audience as well as the reading public in devising many of the incidents in the book. The many touches of melodrama — such as Larry's description of the death of a flier friend during the war, or Isabel's account of the accident in which Sophie loses her husband and child — seem not only meant for the movies but possibly borrowed from them. Similarly, the detailed descriptions of people, places, and things at times seem intended as much to provide the set or costume designer with inspiration as to evoke details necessary for the reader of the novel. By the time of this writing, two film versions of this novel have appeared; by the time Maugham wrote this novel, his other work had served as the basis for many films.[9]

The constant use of coincidence in *The Razor's Edge* is also common to the movies and is somehow more believable there than in the modern novel. In his fiction, Maugham always relies upon coincidence to an extraordinary extent, as a reading of any of his longer works proves. In *The Razor's Edge*, however, one's capacity to believe in such coincidences is given a severe test. Paris is a large city, and when the narrator says at one point early in the novel that by chance he happens upon Larry in a restaurant there, it is difficult to believe him. People do drop in and out of each other's lives (or so one is willing to pretend), but not with such convenience. As with the detail, so with the whole: *The Razor's Edge*, despite its technical finesse, is a novel that is difficult to believe.

It was the last piece of serious long fiction that Maugham produced. It is weak in comparison with his other major works of this kind, and it points up the fact that, by the time he wrote it, he had pretty much exhausted the genre of fiction altogether. He was not to write another novel worth remembering.

5

White Mischief: Maugham's Short Fiction

Very early in his career as a writer, Maugham published a volume of short fiction, but then, for nearly two decades, he abandoned the form, concentrating instead upon drama and longer fiction. In 1920, however, following a trip to the South Seas, he returned to it by writing a classic story—surely his most famous contribution to the genre—the often-anthologized "Rain," which became the basis of a popular play (not by Maugham) and also of a number of films. "Rain" is in many respects a paradigm for what Maugham was to do in the short-story form for the next thirty years or so. The work of a mature writer who knew what he was aiming at, it deserves a close examination for what it can tell about his short-story technique and subject matter.

Of the latter, the first thing that strikes us in "Rain" is the exotic locale, a setting that Maugham staked out early as his own. Other authors in England had written of colonial types in similar settings—Rudyard Kipling and Joseph Conrad come first to mind—but Maugham in his short stories focuses especially on the effect of an exotic environment upon marital (or extramarital) relationships. In his plays (for the most part comedies) Maugham focuses similarly on personal relationships, but generally not in exotic settings.[1] In the short stories, the subject of conjugal fidelity (or infidelity) is transferred from the drawing room to the tropical porch, with its

bamboo furniture and ever-present native servants. E. M.
Forster once said that Sinclair Lewis, with his American characters, had managed "to lodge a piece of a continent in our
imagination";[2] Maugham, with characters who are predomi-
nantly English colonials, manages to do almost the same in
his short fiction, set primarily in the East. The key element of
the characters in "Rain" and elsewhere in the early stories is
less their Englishness, however, than the sense of exile that
they convey. Three of the major characters in "Rain" are in
fact American, but all of the characters, whether American,
English, or European, are in some way exiled from their native land.

For the Davidsons, as well as for the MacPhails, exile is a
matter of choice. For Miss Sadie Thompson, it is a matter of
necessity. In no case, however, is anyone in his or her native
environment. Maugham writes many stories with an English
setting, and many of them are among his finest achievements
in the form. However, it is for the exotic setting that he is best
known, and it is on the whole in stories like these that he
had his greatest success as a writer of short fiction. If we consider Maugham's personal relationship to the English environment, his interest in the exiled is not difficult to understand.

In "Rain," there is on the one hand the grimly puritanical
Reverend Davidson and his wife, for only the latter of whom
one might feel the slightest degree of sympathy by the end of
the story. On the other, there is the slatternly Sadie Thompson, whose attempt at greater moral perfection leads to an
even greater imperfection of personal appearance and who
ends up no more appealing a character than she was at the
beginning, in spite of the unpleasant experience to which she
has been subjected and the sympathy it creates for her in the
reader. In the final analysis, Sadie is not the whore with a
golden heart of popular fiction, nor is she a type of the adul-
teress Christ encounters at the well and to whom the reverend

refers in the story. She is exactly what she is, and what she learns is that the Reverend Davidson is exactly like all the other men she has ever known.

Between these characters (both in the physical and the moral sense) comes the important character of Doctor Mac-Phail. MacPhail serves as the buffer between the Reverend Davidson's overbearing self-righteousness and Sadie Thompson's crumbling, highly vulnerable sense of self. He is described more than once in the story as "timid" or unable to take a firm stand, but when push comes to shove he goes to the governor's office on the behalf of Sadie Thompson. His sympathies go increasingly to her as Reverend Davidson's attempts at her reformation persist. "Live and let live," is Doctor MacPhail's motto; he does not like to be put in the position of having to judge the behavior, moral or otherwise, of other people, but, all the same, he clearly does not side with Reverend Davidson and what he represents.

It is significant in regard to this prevailingly neutral attitude that MacPhail is a physician, for his attitude toward human behavior is much the same as a physician's attitude toward his patients: he notes their behavior, for the most part without passing judgment on it. In other words, he takes the same attitude already noted in Maugham as an author and in the first-person narrators who serve as Maugham's personae in his longer fiction. Doctor MacPhail corresponds to these dispassionate commentators on the human condition.[3] Like them, MacPhail serves to bring the other characters of the story into focus for the reader. It is *through* him that one finds out what Reverend Davidson is hoping to accomplish with Sadie Thompson — or, more properly, through his conversations with Horn or with Davidson or with Sadie herself — not by direct access to the prayer sessions they hold. No major incident of the story is rendered directly for the reader.

This indirect approach, one might argue, is essential to the point of Maugham's story. If one knew precisely what was going on between Sadie and Davidson—in particular what emotions Davidson felt—there would be no surprise at the end. As it is, the reader is given more than a sufficient number of clues that the story will end as it does, beginning with the reference early on to the reverend's "suppressed fire" and "full" and "sensual lips," but these clues come primarily from what others say about the principals and from how Doctor MacPhail reacts to what they say, not from the principals themselves.

Doctor MacPhail thus serves an essential purpose as the character who, by what he observes more than by what he says, brings the behavior of the other characters into focus, both in terms of the plot and of the theme. His place in other Maugham stories may be taken by the narrator through whom characters and events are seen, but, whatever the person, it is more typical of Maugham to tell a story indirectly than to tell it through the unmediated actions of its main characters. In this, "Rain" conforms to the narrative strategy typical of most of Maugham's short stories.

It also conforms to the structure of the typical Maugham story. In his novels Maugham tends at times toward a loose structure, but in his short stories, as in his work for the theater, he follows the classic pattern of the short tale that tends toward a single effect, defined so well in the nineteenth century by Edgar Allan Poe.[4] Without too much distortion, the elements of the classic tale, including turning point and climax, can be perceived in "Rain," though the result of applying such terms to it is to tell only what is already known: that the author builds his story toward Sadie Thompson's final line and the suicide that immediately precedes it. The plot structure of the story thus consists of a series of items of withheld information that can be rendered as questions—why does Sadie not want to return to San Francisco? why is Reverend Davidson so eager to reform her?—and the curve of the plot begins its inevitable descent at that point in the story when Reverend Davidson resolves to break Sadie's will. All else follows in the wake of that ominous decision.

At its best, as in "Rain," this sort of action has a sense of inevitability to it; at its worst, it is merely slick. Seldom, however, is Maugham content simply to sketch a character and not provide a plot by which that character can demonstrate his or her potential for good or evil. Even the most trivial of his stories builds toward some final line or action. The stories end emphatically, and the sense of character they convey is fixed: our initial impression of a character is usually borne out by his or her subsequent behavior. If bad, they may grow slightly worse, but they seldom become better; if good—though their goodness may lead them to folly—they are likely not to turn evil. Good may come of evil actions, or evil of good, but the moral nature of the characters tends to be of a piece.

The cynic always tends to view human nature as fixed, and this perhaps accounts for the feeling one gets in Maugham's best short fiction (as in his long) that his characters are simply fulfilling our expectations of them. In the course of his long career as a writer of short fiction, Maugham varies his subject matter, but seldom his themes, his technique, or his fundamental sense of human nature. The ground might shift to England or to the south of France, but with great consistency the themes remain the selfishness of human motives and the frailty of human will.

For all this consistency of theme, Maugham's stories derive from a variety of sources. The main purpose of most of his travels was to find material to write about. The stories about British colonials in the Far East began after Maugham's first trip there, and all of his subsequent journeys throughout the world produced their own material. Some stories show almost a reportorial approach to their subject matter, as, for instance, "The Letter," which appeared in a collection of 1926 and which sticks very close to the details of a celebrated murder trial in Kuala Lumpur of some twenty-five years earlier.[5]

If the real-life sources of Maugham's subject matter lay in various and sundry places, his literary sources are easier to trace. For his technique of telling a story, Maugham's great model from beginning to end is Guy de Maupassant:

From the age of fifteen whenever I went to Paris I spent most of my afternoons poring over the books in the galleries of the Odeon. I have never passed more enchanted hours. The attendants in their long smocks were indifferent to the people who sauntered about looking at the books and they would let you read for hours without bothering. There was a shelf filled with the works of Guy de Maupassant, but they cost three francs fifty a volume and that was not a sum I was prepared to spend. I had to read as best I could standing up and peering between the uncut pages. Sometimes when no attendant was looking I would hastily cut a page and thus read more conveniently. Fortunately some of them were issued in a cheap edition at seventy-five centimes and I seldom came away without one of these. In this manner, before I was eighteen, I had read all the best stories. It is natural enough that when at that age I began writing stories myself I should unconsciously have chosen those little masterpieces as a model. I might very well have hit upon a worse.

Thus Maugham wrote of his first encounter with the work of the nineteenth-century French master.[6] In contrast with Maupassant, he goes on in the same preface, is the work of Anton Chekhov (and one might add, by extension, many masters of the early twentieth-century short story). Such work emphasizes not action, but character or atmosphere; in contrast with Maugham's ideal short story, little happens in it. Maugham clearly favors the technique of Maupassant, in spite of his clear admiration for Chekhov's gifts.

A second important literary source for Maugham's short

fiction is Poe. In one of his last literary essays Maugham described what Poe's concept of the short story meant to him:

It is a piece of fiction, dealing with a single incident, material or spiritual, that can be read at a sitting; it is original, it must sparkle, excite or impress; and it must have unity of effect or impression. It should move in an even line from its exposition to its close. To write a story on the principles he laid down is not so easy as some think.[7]

If the effect of some of Maugham's tales is less concentrated than some of his pronouncements suggest, one cannot impugn his intention to achieve the desired single effect.

In short fiction as in long, Maugham's technique — especially in the first person — is that of teller of tales. This approach allows him a high degree of narrative flexibility. He can move at will from character to character, shifting viewpoint as he pleases. He can even make use of one or more tellers before getting to the heart of his story. Furthermore, he can do all of this without shifting narrative tone except as the conversation of his characters dictates. If he does not provide a story made aesthetically consistent by its portrayal of the consciousness of a single character (in the manner of Henry James or James Joyce), he does achieve unity through the *tone* in which each story is told. The voice of the narrator, whether in first person or third (or occasionally second, as in one paragraph in "Rain"), thus becomes the most important single unifying element in a Maugham short story.[8]

Atmosphere is another important unifying element. I noted earlier the exotic locale of "Rain." In virtually all of the stories set in the East, descriptive details are important in establishing both mood and character. "Rain" itself provides an obvious example with the physical circumstance suggested by the title. The repeated references to the rain pouring down in the steamy tropical climate add to the sense of imminence created by the small events of the story. Like the celebrated drums constantly in the background in Eugene O'Neill's play *The Emperor Jones* (1920), Maugham's rain suggests the lack of will and obsessiveness often associated with the tropical environment.

Among modern British short stories, Maugham's work stands in the conservative side of a generally conservative lot. Authors like Katherine Mansfield or Virginia Woolf or D. H. Lawrence, whose work was considered innovative when it first appeared, were innovative chiefly in terms of their subject matter or themes. In comparison, continental authors were abandoning traditional forms of short fiction altogether in favor of new, polygeneric forms that fused fiction, poetry, and drama into one.[9] Mainstream twentieth-century British short fiction, as practiced by later writers such as L. P. Hartley, H. E. Bates, or V. S. Pritchett, was neither experimental nor innovative; it is well-crafted work that deals with closely observed patterns of human behavior, with occasional insights gleaned from psychology or myth. Maugham's work, which was essentially nineteenth-century in form, lay somewhat to the right of this solid center. In the end, Maugham's work is closer to that of earlier authors like Rudyard Kipling or Poe—not to mention Maupassant—than it is to the work of most of his contemporaries.

One group of stories in the Maugham canon deserves particular mention—the group, including the celebrated "Mr. Harrington's Washing," collected under the title *Ashenden* (1928). In this volume Maugham brought to fictional life his experiences as a British agent during World War I. Together, these stories achieve sufficient unity of tone and purpose to amount nearly to a novel.[10]

Their central character is the precise opposite of the conventional image of the spy. That image—nurtured in fiction of this period and before by such popular authors as E. Phillips Oppenheim, Anthony Hope, and Ouida—required the spy to be a dashing, romantic figure: handsome, cosmopolitan, ready to do service to the ladies as readily as to his country, native or chosen. Such spies and adventurers were latter-day versions of the Count of Monte Cristo and predecessors to Ian Fleming's popular James Bond.

The Ashenden of Maugham's stories, on the other hand, is reserved, stoic, unromantic; his work is dull, repetitive, even meaningless. He seems to have been chosen for his task because, whatever talent he may have as a writer, he does not know much about espionage and is not likely to wish to distinguish himself by unusually courageous and possibly foolish behavior. He is, in short, more acted upon than active; he lets events (or superiors) dictate his moves rather than attempt to dictate events for himself; and he deliberately avoids romantic contacts the result of which might be the vitiation of his responsibilities. He is the unheroic hero — not a hero at all, but an observer, chosen for his task because of his powers of observation and his distance from others. He is soon to reappear in fiction in the spy novels of Graham Greene and, much later, in the novels of John le Carré.[11]

In Maugham's body of work, Ashenden is remarkable for his contribution to the development of the persona that I have already noted in the longer fiction and that I have suggested came partly as a result of Maugham's desire to distance himself from his alter ego in *Of Human Bondage*. Unheroic or unromantic though he may be, Ashenden is at least not the victim of a self-willed persecution, the slave of emotions that lead him to increasingly neurotic behavior. He is, if anything, above emotions, so that one tends (as with Doctor MacPhail in "Rain") to see events through him. He suggests a dimension of character distinctly different from Philip Carey's, and his next major manifestation — in *Cakes and Ale* — sees him broadened further still.

One of the best features of *Ashenden* (as in much of the short fiction) is its understated style, and one of the best examples of that style comes in the final story of the group, as Anastasia Alexandrovna leads Ashenden to Mr. Harrington's body in revolutionary Russia:

Anastasia Alexandrovna touched Ashenden's arm to draw his attention: sitting on the pavement, her head bent right down to her lap, was a woman and she was dead. A little way on two men had fallen together. They were dead too. The wounded, one supposed, had managed to drag themselves away or their friends had carried them. Then they found Mr. Harrington. His derby had rolled in the gutter. He lay on his face, in a pool of blood, his bald head, with its prominent bones, very white; his neat black coat smeared and muddy. But his hand was clenched tight on the parcel that contained four shirts, two union suits, a pair of pyjamas and four collars. Mr. Harrington had not let his washing go.

The prose in this passage has both tautness and immediacy, and the final line (typical of a Maugham story) provides a satisfying touch. If one is fond of this kind of fiction, one ends by wishing that Maugham had decided to come back to it again.

In the end, the Ashenden stories notwithstanding, one probably remembers best the Maugham short stories that, like "Rain," have exotic settings. These stories continue the account of the British imperial experience begun by Kipling, carrying it into its decadence and ultimate corruption, the last to be memorialized in fiction much later on by writers like Paul Scott (in his *Raj Quartet*). Maugham's short stories also continue the tradition of the nineteenth-century tale. "No author," Angus Wilson observed of Maugham in a preface to a selection of his short stories, "has more cleverly converted his defects into assets, not only by his assumption of the classic and stoic framework of life (through which the lost romantic is only occasionally allowed yearningly to peer), but far more by the perfection of his craft, imposing upon his carefully limited material an even more rigorous form, and then becoming so completely master of this highly artificial technique that his stories appear to flow with the ease and simplicity of ordinary, everyday muddled life."[12] In the best of the short fiction, through such means, Maugham achieved a vision and tone uniquely his. If he had written nothing else, his best short stories would guarantee him a place of note in English literary history.

6

Wit's End:
Maugham's Work for the Theater

In *The Summing Up*, at the beginning of his discussion of the important elements of drama, Maugham remarks that a prose play is "scarcely less ephemeral than a news sheet." The note of prophecy in this remark, in relationship to his own plays, was not lost on Maugham, because it is his plays that gave rise to it: he gave up writing for the stage because he determined that such work had little lasting value. It had served a purpose in his career—that of establishing him as an author of prominence—and it had definitely rewarded him well, but in the end Maugham never felt totally at home in the theater and abandoned it after 1933 without regret. Were he alive today, he would not be surprised to find that most of his plays have been relegated to the library shelf, with only a few showing signs of more-permanent life.[1]

Maugham's approach to the drama was the same as his general approach to the writing of fiction: that of the craftsman and professional who knows what he must do in order to satisfy the requirements of the genre in which he is working and the tastes of his audience. Elsewhere in *The Summing Up*, Maugham notes that a play represents a collaboration between the author, the actors, and the audience (also, he adds somewhat reluctantly, the director), but clearly the most important of these elements, in his analysis, is the audience: "All the best dramatists have written with their eye on it and though they have more often spoken of it with contempt than with good will they have known that they were dependent on it. It is the public that pays, and if it is not pleased with the entertainment that is offered it, stays away."

While the great innovators of the modern drama—Ibsen, Chekhov, Strindberg, Pirandello, and Brecht—certainly never lost sight of the fact that they were writing for an audience, they also just as certainly did not write with the tastes of the audience foremost in their minds. Rather, they molded the public to their view of drama, creating their own audience, even when this involved a great deal of personal travail. By contrast, Maugham was a popular dramatist who wrote plays to suit the requirements of the commercial theater. He did variations on a commonly appreciated theme—primarily comedies that turned upon the question of whether someone would marry (or stay married) or not—and reserved innovation, to the extent that he practiced it, for his last few plays, by which point he no longer cared whether he retained his audience or not.

If this sounds deprecating, it should be kept in mind that throughout history, most of world drama conforms to Maugham's dictum that the audience is the most important element in the theatrical mixture. It should also be kept in mind that in the particular form in which Maugham specialized—a form derived from sophisticated drawing-room comedy of the English school—he clearly excelled. For some twenty-five years his work was among the best the English stage had to offer.

Maugham began writing for the Edwardian stage and ended his career during the Great Depression. His work reflects the changing tastes of audiences during this transitional period in British drama. Much of that work is comedy, and much of that comedy turns upon the question of marriage. Furthermore, almost all of the plays are focused upon female characters. Beginning with Maugham's first real success as a playwright, *Lady Frederick* (1903; first produced 1907), his plots center on his heroines' relationships and on decisions in their personal lives. The whole plot of *Lady Frederick* turns on the question: whom will Lady Frederick, a woman of somewhat doubtful reputation, marry? In *Penelope* (1908; 1909), the protagonist remains tied to her unfaithful husband, who shows by the end of the play that he loves her once again. *Our Betters* (1915; 1917) asserts the importance of marital fidelity less directly, but no less conclusively, when Bessie, the American girl whose sister has become the mistress of a wealthy Englishman, decides against marriage with an English lord because she has seen her sister decline as part of the English aristocracy. *Caesar's Wife* (1918; 1919) sees Violet, in the manner of Penelope, reunited with her husband by the end of the play. There are exceptions—for instance, in *Caroline* (1915; 1916) the main character, as the subtitle of the play suggests, remains "unattainable," her husband missing or dead—but in general these plays support the notion of love through marriage, a convention of the Edwardian, not to mention the Victorian, stage.[2]

The Circle (1919; 1921) differs thematically from most of these plays, yet at the same time it typifies in most respects Maugham's whole approach to drama. It is also, of all his plays, the one most completely alive today.

The title of *The Circle* tells much about its subject and theme, for a circle consists of a single, continuous line whose end is its beginning. As a geometric form, it is perfect; as a symbol, it suggests action that repeats itself. Indeed, the action of *The Circle* is a repetition of events that happened previously, but with a difference that makes them, as the original subtitle of the play suggests, "modern." Elizabeth and Teddie do not simply repeat the experience of some thirty years earlier of Lady Kitty and Lord Porteus; they do it their way, in the modern manner. Their decision becomes their

own, as Porteus suggests in one of the key speeches of the
play: "No one can learn by the experience of another because
no circumstances are quite the same."

Elizabeth is married to Arnold Champion-Cheney, MP,
but is in love with the much less wealthy, much more aggres-
sive Edward Lutton, a planter who hopes to make his fortune
in the Federated Malay States. Elizabeth must ultimately
choose between the loveless security of her relationship with
Arnold, and the much more exciting, though much more
insecure, alliance with Teddie. For Arnold, the situation is
especially painful, because his mother, Lady Kitty, left his
father for Lord Porteus and has not been back to see him
since.

As the play opens, all the parties to the earlier elopement
appear on the scene at the stately family home of the Champi-
on-Cheneys, including Arnold's father, who chooses to visit
at the very time Elizabeth has extended an invitation to Lady
Kitty and Lord Porteus to spend some time there. His presence completes the equations among the characters important
to the complications of the plot: Elizabeth with Lady Kitty,
Teddie with Lord Porteus, and Arnold with his father. As
Elizabeth and Arnold are trying to adjust to the tension
aroused by these visitors, Elizabeth realizes that she is the
object of the affection of Teddie Lutton. In the scenes that
ensue, Arnold at first completely resists Elizabeth's declared
intention to leave him, then, prompted by his father (who
speaks from his own experience), tries to make Elizabeth feel
so guilty about what she is doing that she will desist. Ultimately, however, the affection that Elizabeth feels for Teddie
is great enough to overcome any scruples she may have, and,
aided and abetted by the lovers of an older generation, she
and Teddie escape into the night to begin their own adventures together.

If the final scene of the play suggests the similarity between Elizabeth's decision and Kitty's, much else in the play

suggests how different the two women are. In that difference lies much of the point, and poignancy, of Maugham's comedy. At first Elizabeth imagines Kitty to be a romantic figure who surprised her husband by running off with his best friend. This impression is tarnished by the reality of Kitty grown old and the revelation of how difficult it has been for her and her lover through the years. Still, Elizabeth's approach to leaving Arnold is markedly different from Kitty's way of leaving his father; in the difference one sees why Kitty can't live without lipstick, while Elizabeth never uses it. Elizabeth, when she realizes that she is in love with Teddie, confronts Arnold with the fact very openly and candidly; it is Arnold who is devious in dealing with the situation. Furthermore, what Elizabeth responds to in Teddie is *his* openness and candor. "It's you I love, not what you look like," he says to her. "And it's not only love; love be blowed! It's that I *like* you so tremendously." Unlike the older Kitty—and unlike the women of many of Maugham's earlier plays—Elizabeth is incapable of behaving in a devious manner.

Elizabeth and Teddie also form an exception to the typically unequal heterosexual relationships in the work of Maugham. Elizabeth gives up a great deal to run away with Teddie, but at the same time she gains a measure of self-respect and independence that is significantly lacking in her married relationship. Teddie promises her little, but it is clear that she feels what she has with Arnold is suffocating her: "I don't want luxury. You don't know how sick I am of all this beautiful furniture," she tells Kitty early in act 3. "These overdecorated houses are like a prison in which I can't breathe." It is Lady Kitty, however, who strikes the ultimate note of realism on the subject when she says, "Woman will only be the equal of man when she earns her living in the same way that he does." Kitty is willing to risk that necessity, for Teddie promises her nothing.

Between Arnold and Teddie there is a contrast just as

deep as the one between Elizabeth and Lady Kitty. Arnold is interested in old furniture and a political career; he is as conservative in his viewpoint on life as presumably he is conservative in his politics. Marriage completes his personal circle, and his desire to keep Elizabeth from leaving has as much to do with his personal ambition (and his sense that history should not repeat itself in his family) as it does with his affection for her. It is clear in fact that the affection of Arnold and Elizabeth for each other has long since cooled to the level of familiarity without ardor.

Teddie on the other hand is interested not in marriage but in Elizabeth herself. He is bold enough to have gone to the colonies to make his fortune, and the ultimate outcome of that venture, like the ultimate outcome of his relationship with Elizabeth, remains very much in question. Teddie is a positive version of Edward Barnard, who, in Maugham's short story of this same period, went to the South Seas and decided not to return. Teddie may not return either, for, like Elizabeth, he seems to find the English environment stultifying. Unlike Edward Barnard, however, Teddie may be successful in making his fortune.

If the tendency of Maugham's earlier comedies was toward a decision in favor of marriage, *The Circle* reflects the general tendency of British comedy of the twenties toward less conventional outcomes. Elizabeth and Teddie are not part of the Bright Set to emerge in the later twenties in the work of Noel Coward and others who became famous for representing the style of life of postwar British youth (for one thing they are too old to be counted in this category), but their decision to run off has about it the same no-nonsense toughness associated with the characters in Coward's work. Like Constance and her husband in *The Constant Wife*, Teddie and Elizabeth work out their own version of destiny. In doing so, they are at the same time more open and more bold than

Lady Kitty and Lord Porteus, their immediate predecessors in such a venture in the play.

In many respects, however, the characters of *The Circle* are of a piece with those of Maugham's earlier comedies, as the play in which they occur is in many respects characteristic of Maugham's established brand of comedy. The characters of *The Circle* (with the exception of Teddie) are both titled and wealthy. Money is important to them, but as a means to maintain their way of life, not as an end in itself. The male characters are not, for the most part, financiers or men on the way up the ladder. They are at the top, or near it, and trying to stay there. Their careers, if they have visible ones, are in the respectable professions or in politics, but their careers are not of first importance in these plays: the focus is rather upon their personal relationships, the comedies reaching their points of crisis over decisions to marry or not to marry, to leave one's spouse or stay. Although the wives and mistresses of these plays are concerned with romantic intrigues and assignations, as well as with the right hat or gown, they are on the whole more important than the males. The focus of the plays is on their reactions and development, and they determine the course of events more than the male characters do. Maugham's comedies, in short, reflect in their characters as in their structure most of the qualities of the English drawing-room comedy.[3]

The fundamentally aristocratic nature of the characters and the emphasis of the plays upon their personal affairs are both characteristic of this kind of comedy. So is the tendency—not overbearingly strong in *The Circle*, but certainly noticeable—toward aphorism in the writing: "It's very unfair to expect a politician to live in private up to the statements he makes in public" (Mrs. Shenstone to Elizabeth in act 1); "I always reserve to myself the privilege of changing my mind. It's the only one elderly gentlemen share with pretty women"

(Arnold's father to Elizabeth in act 1); "The tragedy of love isn't death or separation. One gets over them. The tragedy of love is indifference" (Lady Kitty to Elizabeth in act 3). These and other lines like them typify the dialogue of Maugham's comedies and of drawing-room comedy in general. It is less important what the characters have to say than how they say it, and such statements form an important part of the thematic underpinning of the play, on which its action, however related to the wisdom they suggest, is built. Maugham was especially noted for his skill at this kind of dialogue, which audiences and critics alike expected in this comic form.

The plot line of drawing-room comedy is frequently complicated but it must always be clearly and neatly resolved by the end of the final act. The pleasure is in seeing how, with all the complications, the playwright gets us there. In Maugham's comedies the twists of the plot are not extraordinarily complex, but, as in *The Circle*, one does not know until the end of the play what the outcome will be. In this respect as well as in others Maugham's comedies are related to the *pièce bien faite* (the well-made play) of the French tradition, an influence that one would expect to see reflected in the work of an author much indebted in other ways to French literature.

The well-made play follows the pattern of exposition, complication, and resolution, with the climax of the play, the ultimate point of revelation, coming at the very end, often in the final line. Augustin-Eugène Scribe defined the genre. Victorien Sardou's *Tosca*, made familiar by Giacomo Puccini's opera, is a good example of it, and so, in British drama, is Arthur Wing Pinero's *The Second Mrs. Tanqueray* (1895). As serious drama, the well-made play takes the form of melodrama. As comedy, it tends toward farce. If Maugham's work does not follow precisely the pattern of such plays, it nevertheless shares with them a sufficient number of characteristics to make analysis in such terms informative. His serious dramas all have the marks of melodrama—certainly one reason

for their popularity—and many of his early comedies are in
fact best described as farces. In the end, however, it is English
drawing-room comedy, more than the French tradition, that
provides the model for Maugham's comedies.[4]

The master of English drawing-room comedy was Oscar
Wilde. In such plays as *Lady Windermere's Fan* (1893) and
The Importance of Being Earnest (1899) (his greatest dramatic achievement) he used the form (with appropriate touches of
the *pièce bien faite*) to create a new comedy of manners,
reviving a type of play not significant in England since the
eighteenth century. So individual was Wilde's achievement in
the form that it was to a large extent inimitable, but it did
encourage the popularity of drawing-room comedy in the
nineties; such comedy later became a staple of Edwardian
theater. By the time Maugham began to write plays, it was
only natural, given his desire for commercial success, that he
should write plays of this kind.

Of the other comedies of Maugham it is probably *The
Constant Wife* (1926) that would best hold the boards today.
In this stylish comedy (Maugham's next-to-last effort in this
particular vein) Constance Middleton and her husband John
take the flippant view of marital fidelity soon to be immortal-
ized in Noel Coward's *Private Lives* (1929). After a series of
complications derived from John's affair with another woman, Constance—now with the independent means that Lady
Kitty in *The Circle* tells Elizabeth are essential to a woman's
independence—has her own fling, but leaves with the understanding, reached at the end of the final act, that she can
return. "You are the most maddening, wilful, capricious,
wrong-headed, delightful and enchanting woman man was
ever cursed with having for a wife," John says in the final
speech. "Yes, damn you, come back." Constance, unlike Elizabeth, wants independence and marriage at the same time
and manages to achieve both.

*   *   *

If Maugham is noted today chiefly for his comedies, one must not forget that he wrote more serious plays as well. *Our Betters* and *The Circle* are both comedies with an edge of seriousness that nearly carries them over the line. Other plays begin in that other terrain. Part of Maugham's impatience with theater came from his feeling that he would have to continue writing what his audience had come to expect of him, which for the most part meant comedies. This growing impatience led him to his decision to stop writing plays altogether.

Having made that decision, Maugham was equally determined that he would write four more: "I had been thinking of them all for a good many years; I had done nothing about them because I did not think they would please. . . . I wrote these four plays in the order in which I expected them to be increasingly unsuccessful." The first two—*The Sacred Flame* (1928) and *The Breadwinner* (1930)—turned out to be fairly successful. The last two—*For Services Rendered* (1932) and *Sheppey* (1933)—did not succeed. The intentions of their author were achieved. As a group these plays are interesting for what they tell about Maugham as a dramatist not aiming to please—that is, not writing with any particular concern for the financial success of his play.

Each of these plays attempts to do something different from what Maugham was best known for as a playwright. In *The Sacred Flame*, a play about the tragic circumstances surrounding the death of a pilot paralyzed in World War I, Maugham tried to escape from what he saw as the increasing tyranny of naturalistic dialogue in prose drama. "In certain passages," Maugham writes of the play in his introduction to the *Collected Plays*, "I tried, quite deliberately, to make my characters use not the words and expressions that they would have used in real life on the spur of the moment and in the give and take of conversation, but words and expressions that they might have used if they had had time to set their thoughts in order." Thus Mrs. Tabret to Stella in act 2: "I could never bring myself to teach my children what I couldn't myself believe. When they were little and I used to sit in the evenings in our house and look at the multitudinous stars sweeping across the blue sky of India and thought of what we are, so transitory and so insignificant, and yet with such a capacity for suffering, such a passion for beauty, I was overwhelmed by the mystery and the immensity of the universe." Or Nurse Wayland, at a moment of high emotion, again to Stella, in act 3: "No. No. My love for that poor boy was as pure and as spiritual as my love for God. There was never a shadow of self in it. My love was compassion and Christian charity. I never asked anything but to be allowed to serve and tend him." Rather than finding this dialogue more expressive than the customary dialogue of the day, critics found it stilted (not to say stale), and Maugham did not attempt it again.

The Breadwinner, Maugham's last comedy, takes the situation of *The Constant Wife*—that of a wife who realizes that her marriage is no longer working and wants to do something about it—and applies it to the husband. Charles Battle (the last name suggests something of his spirit, and the first calls to mind another Charles, also a stockbroker, in *The Moon and Sixpence*) realizes that his marriage has gone flat and his relationship with his children has become pointless, so he leaves both rather than prolong the institution of marriage that he no longer values. Like the decision of Charles Strickland, Charles Battle's is irrevocable, and the end of the play sees him leaving for his new life.

For Services Rendered is Maugham's statement on the effects of World War I, at least insofar as they can be felt by a small group of characters in a provincial English town. In 1929 R. C. Sheriff's *Journey's End* had been an immensely successful portrait of life in the trenches, and in the next year, Noel Coward's *Cavalcade*, a chronicle of an English family during the years from 1899 to 1929, dealt with the effects of the war on the people back home. In *For Services Rendered*

Maugham shows that for those who stayed at home the re-
wards of service were neuroticism or madness, with Eva's
cracked rendition of the national anthem, at the end of the
final act, an ironic commentary on the complacency of her
father and mother (and also perhaps a comment on the use of
the same anthem, in a patriotic context, at the end of *Cavalcade*).

Sheppey, the final play of Maugham's last four, deals
with the familiar situation of the man of modest means who
comes into money—in this case by way of a winning ticket in
the Irish Sweepstakes. What effect will this small fortune have
on the lower-middle-class barber who gives his name to the
play? All the money seems to inspire in Sheppey—whose
daughter has the same selfishness that is seen so often in
children in Maugham's plays (an anticipation perhaps of
Maugham's later attitude toward his own daughter)—is the
desire to give it away to the poor and needy, the downtrodden
and distraught. In a play that begins as a straightforward,
low-keyed piece of naturalism with comic overtones, Sheppey's second-act conversion comes as too much of a surprise,
but even so, the appearance in the final act of Death, come to
claim him as her own, has a gripping dramatic effect and
indicates the distance Maugham has come from the sort of
play that made him famous. The final scene of *Sheppey* represents a return to one of the earliest forms of drama, allegory,
and reflects Maugham's unhappiness with the strictures of
realistic theater. "I sighed for the liberty of fiction," he writes
in *The Summing Up*, "and I thought with pleasure of the
lonely reader who was willing to listen to all I had to say and
with whom I could effect an intimacy that I could never hope
for in the garish publicity of the theater."

What was Maugham's achievement in the theater? He
produced in his thirty-two plays probably the most significant
body of work in English drama after George Bernard Shaw
and before Noel Coward, yet comparison with the achieve-

ment of the first of these playwrights, at least, can only be damaging to Maugham. Nowhere in Maugham's work for the theater does one see the brilliance, the wit, or the intellectual energy that make Shaw's work, particularly after the turn of the century, so compelling a part of theater to this day. By comparison, Maugham's work seems pale, dated, and trivial, even when, as in the very best of it, all of its elements work. Shaw used theatrical effect—especially in his earlier plays, but also in such later ones as *Androcles and the Lion*—in the service of ideas, a procedure that energized otherwise conventional forms and made them seem, if not new, at least renewed by his touch. Maugham on the other hand more often used theatrical effect for its own sake to engage the audience and never produced any drama that was in any sense intellectually compelling. One could argue indeed that the more he tried to produce such work, as in his last plays, the less he succeeded as a dramatist. Maugham frankly sought in drama something to which Shaw paid far less attention, and often eschewed: popularity with the audience.

Coward, like Maugham, actively sought to be a popular dramatist. Like Maugham, he took various commercial forms of drama, serious as well as comic, and eventually made them his own, including the form of high comedy at which Maugham excelled. All of Coward's plays show a strong sense of theatrical effect and artifice and an equally strong sense of what audiences looked for. Coward's work, however—in particular his comedies—has managed to maintain its popularity to this day while Maugham's for the most part has not. Coward's comedy may reflect the style of a period, but it also speaks to us in our own; Maugham's comedy speaks for its time, but not so well for ours.

The difference between the work of these popular dramatists perhaps tells us more than their similarities, at least insofar as Maugham's achievement is concerned. The difference lies in Coward's greater individuality as well as in his greater separation from Edwardian forms. In structure and content most of Maugham's dramatic work conforms to the conventions of a bygone era; Coward's is much looser in structure and tone ("the average talk," Maugham was to describe Coward's dialogue, "with its hesitations, mumblings and repetitions, of average people"), hence in a sense more modern. It is also, in a way Maugham's never is, more individual: Coward not only wrote for the theater, but also wrote parts for himself in his best plays. For this reason, as well as for their tone, Coward's comedies achieve an individuality that Maugham's never manage and in fact never aim for. Maugham remains outside his work for the theater and, though it may at times share certain themes or attitudes with his fiction, it is in the end far less individual. When one thinks of Maugham's "voice," it is of the fiction — or nonfiction — that he wrote, not the plays.

At the same time one must give Maugham his due as a dramatist. Even at this late date, in plays like *The Circle* and *The Constant Wife*, one can appreciate what he does with a now-extinct comic form. One must also never underestimate the power of a good revival: many plays by many playwrights have been written off as outdated or no longer of interest to the general audience, only to be seen in a different light after they have been touched by the hand of the right director or acted by the right star.

7

The Lion of the Villa Mauresque:
The Essays and Memoirs

In the last several decades of his writing career, the essay and memoir became increasingly important genres for Maugham. One of his earliest books was a work of nonfiction, a travel book about Spain, *The Land of the Blessed Virgin* (1905); it was followed in the twenties and thirties by several other books of the same type, along with numerous literary prefaces and introductions. With the publication of *The Summing Up* in 1938, however, Maugham broke new ground: here was a work that was both autobiography and essay, written with a clarity and preciseness that made it immediately appealing in terms of its style. Never again did Maugham achieve quite the same balance of form and content in such a book, though each of the later works of the same kind — *Strictly Personal* (1941), a memoir of the fall of France, and *Purely for My Pleasure* (1962), an account of Maugham's art collecting — has something to recommend it. In many ways *The Summing Up* was the best work Maugham was to do in the last years of his life; it also represents the triumph of the essay voice toward which he leaned in his writing from the beginning and which he employed for narrative purposes in his last major work of fiction, *The Razor's Edge*.

Early in *The Summing Up* Maugham declares his purpose to the reader: "In this book I am going to try to sort out my thoughts on the subjects that have chiefly interested me during the course of my life. But such conclusions as I have come to have drifted about my mind like the wreckage of a foundered ship on a restless sea. It has seemed to me that if I set them down in some sort of order I should see for myself more distinctly what they really were and so might get some kind of coherence in them." If the reader expects a book of intimate revelations, however, he is soon disappointed: Maugham disavows in the very first sentence of the book the notion that he is writing either an autobiography or a book of recollections (though in fact he does both). His purpose truly is to sort out his *thoughts*, and it is soon clear that *The Summing Up* represents an intellectual and artistic history more than a personal one. The author laments the difficulty of writing in the first person—"I have been held back . . . by the irksomeness of setting down my own thoughts in my own person"; "Long habit has made it more comfortable for me to speak through the creatures of my invention"—but, at the same time, he presents a persona as carefully cultivated as any to be encountered in his fiction. "The celebrated develop a technique to deal with the persons they come across. They show the world a mask, often an impressive one, but take care to conceal their real selves"—this observation, also from early in the book, describes precisely the presentation of the self that Maugham manages in this impersonal memoir.

If the autobiographical portions of *The Summing Up* conceal more than they reveal, providing at best only a sketchy view of Maugham's life (or those portions of it that he chose to make known to the world), the portions of the book that deal with the process of literary creation are much more forthright. Maugham says what everyone knew: he approached writing as a craft in which the most important elements are the perseverance of the writer and his sense of what his audience expects of him. Maugham's career as playwright, fiction writer, and essayist was built on this approach. Other elements of the process are consonant with the first two. The writing of fiction and drama requires a strong sense of probability ("My fancy, never very strong, has been hampered by my sense of probability. I have painted easel pictures, not frescoes"). Writing is a craft that the beginning professional acquires at the expense of his public but that can be acquired only if the taste of that public is considered. Writing is a means of earning a living, a respectable profession like that of medicine or the law ("I am a writer as I might have been a doctor or a lawyer. It is so pleasant a profession that it is not surprising if a vast number of persons adopt it who have no qualifications for it"). These and similar ideas reflect Maugham's view of the maker of literature and his place in society. This is a far cry from either the romantic notion of the artist with divine aspirations or the avant-garde notion, prevalent especially in the early decades of this century, of the artist as an antibourgeois out to upset the status quo; Maugham's view of the making of literature largely excludes the notions of divinity and rebellion. To Maugham the artist is a craftsman whose work has a price on it; he is impatient with the amateur or the dilettante and has the greatest respect for the writer capable of producing the oeuvre — the extensive body of work that is the product of a lifetime.

In the end, whatever its disadvantages or pitfalls, the profession of author gives its practitioner the important quality of "spiritual freedom":

To him life is a tragedy and by his gift of creation he enjoys the catharsis, the purging of pity and terror, which Aristotle tells us is the object of art. For his sins and his follies, the unhappiness that befalls him, his unrequited love, his physical defects, illness, privation, his hopes abandoned, his griefs, humiliations, everything is transformed by his power into materials and by writing it he can overcome it.

"The artist," Maugham concludes, "is the only free man."[1]

On the matter of literary genres, *The Summing Up* confirms Maugham's preference for prose fiction, short or long, over the drama. While there are illuminating passages on the writing of drama, in particular on Maugham's last plays, it is clear that the theater represented for him too great an accommodation to conventions. When he abandoned it, he did so because he no longer needed the income it provided, but also because he realized that he needed the greater freedom provided by fiction. He felt confined by the conventions of drama and by the degree of realism it persisted in demanding of what he felt was essentially an artificial form. Like Stephen Dedalus in Joyce's *A Portrait of the Artist as a Young Man*, Maugham in the end finds drama the least personal form of literature; he yearns instead for a form that allows him to exercise a greater measure of freedom to speak more directly for — and from — himself to the reader.

The Summing Up is concerned chiefly with literature — the making of it, the evaluation of it, the various forms of it — and with brief accounts of important incidents in Maugham's life that contributed to his work, such as the circumstances of his childhood and youth and his work in Russia during World War I. The concluding sections of the book, however, represent a philosophical statement by one who had been interested throughout his life not only in literature in all its forms, but also in more abstract things. One must remember that it was not simply Maugham's desire to leave England that led him to Germany as a young man, but also his interest in philosophy. That interest was to last throughout his life, figuring prominently in *The Summing Up* as it does in *The Razor's Edge*.

If Larry Darrell's philosophy, as it is recounted in chapter 6 of *The Razor's Edge*, is a combination of idealism and fatalism, the philosophy that Maugham sketches in the final sections of *The Summing Up* combines determinism and

skepticism, with emphasis on the latter. This philosophy corresponds in abstract terms to the cynical viewpoint that is
found so often in the fiction. There is no real point to life,
merely a pattern that is created to try to give it meaning. God
is an invention to explain the existence of evil, but evil will
exist even if the existence of God is not acknowledged. Ultimately, the greatest meaning in life is found in art, and the
qualities of art that mean most are the traditional ones—
truth, beauty, and goodness. In the final analysis, however,
truth and beauty are relative and goodness is seldom attained.
On this point, Maugham ends his discussion on a Voltairean
note: "The beauty of life . . . is nothing but this, that each
should act in conformity with his nature and his business."

If there is any point to life at all, that point is personal or
selfish. The pattern that one imposes on reality has little
general application, and the plain man (to whom Maugham
frequently refers) will find little to learn from it:

If anyone should ask me what is the use or sense of this pattern I
should have to answer, none. It is merely something I have imposed
on the senselessness of life because I am a novelist. For my own
satisfaction, for my amusement and to gratify what feels to me like
an organic need, I have shaped my life in accordance with a certain
design, with a beginning, a middle and an end, as from people I
have met here and there I have constructed a play, a novel or a short
story. We are the product of our natures and environment. I have
not made the pattern I should have liked to make, but merely that
which seemed feasible.

The pattern that Maugham imposes upon his material in
The Summing Up is both chronological and thematic. The
sections of reminiscence in the book follow roughly the order
in which they took place in Maugham's life; the more abstract
sections follow a similar pattern, in line with Maugham's

artistic and intellectual development. In the end, he creates what seems almost like a book of essays tied together by certain common themes, a form he attempted earlier in the thirties, with less success, in the book on Spain entitled *Don Fernando* (1935). Perhaps it is the personal element of *The Summing Up* (however impersonally rendered) that makes it succeed where the other book did not, but it shares with it a style of writing.

The inspiration for the essay style of *The Summing Up* comes from English literature of the late seventeenth and early eighteenth centuries, and the stylistic qualities to which Maugham aspired in writing it, as in all such work that he did, were those of lucidity, simplicity, and euphony. After writing *The Land of the Blessed Virgin* in the lush, hothouse style of the 1890s and the turn of the century, Maugham realized how inappropriate that style of writing was for him and undertook a systematic study of the writing of the Augustan period, especially that of Swift. Finding Swift's style ultimately too perfect—Maugham likens it in *The Summing Up* to a French canal bordered with poplars: "You go on and on and presently you are a trifle bored"—he went on to discover Dryden, who was much more to his taste, and then Hazlitt, who, though of a later time, had the same qualities in his prose that Maugham admired in Dryden's. Gradually Maugham came to appreciate the advantages of a clear prose style of conversational quality and attempted to achieve it in his work ever afterward.

In December 1934 he also became reacquainted with Eddie Marsh, who in his lifetime served as private secretary both to Sir Winston Churchill and Neville Chamberlain and who, until his death in 1953, gave editorial advice to Maugham. Marsh was that rare figure, the dilettante who could be practical. His influence was first felt in Maugham's work in the pages of *Don Fernando*. Marsh was particularly helpful to Maugham in the matter of clichés, which

Maugham often used deliberately to ingratiate himself with the reader.[2] Under Marsh's influence, Maugham managed to maintain a suitable simplicity while avoiding the painfully obvious phrase. Marsh's influence—like many such influences in the work of professional writers—merely served to confirm the direction that Maugham was already moving in, not to direct it. In the best work of Maugham's last several decades, it was the essay voice that predominated, and Marsh helped Maugham to perfect it.

Strictly Personal consists almost entirely of reminiscence. Specifically, it is a memoir of the fall of France, recounted from the standpoint of one who had lived there for some years and who, with others of his class, was forced to leave in some haste after the German advance. The year before, Maugham had published a book of reportage called *France at War* in which he took the position, not unique at the time, that France could withstand an attack from its traditional enemy; he was sure the Maginot Line would hold. *Strictly Personal* is an engaging about-face to that position—a personal view of what happened when the French strategy failed. It is one of the most pleasing of Maugham's minor works, conveying unsentimentally a fine sense of a particular time and place. In style, it is deliberately understated, as if to bring the events it describes within human compass. Its account of the long and unpleasant trip by coal boat to England by way of North Africa is a gem:

I think the oddest person on board was one who would have been vastly surprised if anyone had told him that he was in any way unusual. This was the butler of a neighbour of mine on Cap Ferrat whom I had persuaded to come with me. A tall gray-haired man, of dignified presence, with a long, thin face, and a manner which was at once affable and distant. Because I was a friend of his mistress he saw fit to give me the sort of attention he would have done if I had been a visitor in her house; at the crack of dawn he brought me a cup of tea, he brushed my grimy clothes and, though I was entirely indifferent to it, shined my shoes. Though we sat on the iron deck to eat our meals, he waited on us with the same ceremony as he would have used at a dinner party. Nothing disturbed him. On the afternoon when we had the [submarine] scare of which I spoke just now, he came up to his mistress, who was standing with me at the side trying to see the periscope, and said: "Will you have your tea now, madam, or will you wait till the excitement subsides?"

In addition to *Strictly Personal* and *Purely for My Pleasure*, which is remarkable chiefly as the last of Maugham's works published in his lifetime, *A Writer's Notebook* falls into the same category of writing. In this volume of 1949 Maugham provided excerpts from his notebooks, but, in typical fashion, edited them carefully to make sure they revealed no more of himself than he chose to make known. Organized chronologically by year of entry, the notes show the reader the germ of various stories, including those in *Ashenden*, but give little sense of the personal life of the author. As ever, Maugham was protective of himself, creating a persona for the benefit of the reader, but keeping the real Maugham well hidden.

Given his appreciation for literary craftsmanship and his conception of writing as a profession, Maugham's personal literary tastes were scarcely surprising. Those tastes were conservative, though the reading that formed them was catholic. Widely as he would read, Maugham returned to the values in literature that he cherished at the outset and practiced in his own work: a strong story line, a feeling for form, and a certain sense of style. As to literary experimentation in its various forms, Maugham was unfriendly from virtually the beginning; after the briefest of flirtations with the purple style of the 1890s, he chose a plain style and never felt inclined, either as writer or as reader, toward the complexities characteristic of so much of twentieth-century literature.

As one reads the various essays, prefaces, and introductions that make up the corpus of Maugham's critical work (including also the literary sections of *The Summing Up*), one is struck by the breadth of his reading. Here truly is someone who read widely and who found from early in his life both respite and nourishment in literature (Philip, in *Of Human Bondage*, through his reading provided "himself with a refuge from all the distress of life"). Here also is someone whose taste in literature remained remarkably consistent. From the early reading in classic English authors on, Maugham sought in literature a coherence he knew from his own experience that life frequently lacked. As with the game of bridge (of which he was inordinately fond), so with his favorite reading: it provided for him "a certain design." In no way, however, did his reading exclude the pain of life; that pain was simply made more bearable by the fact that his favorite authors gave it form.

It is perhaps this very sense of form—of the pattern in events as Maugham developed it in his own work—that made him so successful a writer of drama and short stories. There are writers for whom the narrow compass is too confining, whose talents come to fruition only when, like Dostoyevski's or Tolstoy's, they are stretched to their utmost limits. As a writer, Maugham realized that he did not have this kind of talent, however much he might appreciate it as a reader. His own talent lay primarily in tidier things, smaller creations, in which motive and line of development are simpler. Hence his comment that he painted easel pictures, not frescoes; hence also his appreciation of the craftsmanship in literature and his suspicion of the experimentation—the formlessness, as he saw it—in so much of modern literature.

As a literary essayist his technique is biographical and discursive. He conveys a strong sense of the life of the writers he deals with and its relationship to their work; he does not ordinarily set out to prove a thesis, but rather to give the

reader, through anecdote and example, a feeling for the subject. This approach to a literary subject matter — which may
seem impressionistic to a reader of our day and certainly, at
times, opinionated — is typical of literary essayists of the late
nineteenth and early twentieth centuries. The typical approach to the interpretation of a work of literature was by way
of the biography of its author. When there is obvious sympathy on the part of the essayist for the life and work of the
subject, the approach works best. In Maugham's case, the
essay on Edmund Burke in *The Vagrant Mood* (1952) provides an excellent example of just such a degree of sympathy
and a corresponding degree of illumination.

This essay also provides an example of Maugham's sensi-
tivity to style, a subject on which he frequently touches in his
literary essays. Style is the real subject of the essay on Burke,
as it is of the delightful "Prose and Dr. Tillotson," in *Points of
View* (1958), about a cleric who had been chaplain at Lin-
coln's Inn in the latter part of the seventeenth century and a
writer in the plain style to which Maugham was always attracted. In these essays and others like them, as in the pages
of *The Summing Up*, Maugham asserts the importance of
writing with simplicity and in the style of one's age. As he
puts it in his National Book League Lecture of 1951, "The
Writer's Point of View": "For my part I prefer plain writing
and I think it is more in the spirit of our day. But to write
plainly is not a gift of nature: it has to be learnt. Of course
one must write in the manner of one's own period. To try to
write like the masters of the early eighteenth century would
be absurd, but all the same to study them carefully cannot fail
to help the modern writer to write well, clearly, simply and
precisely."

Some of Maugham's essays deal, not with individual authors, but with genres of work that Maugham enjoyed. The
detective story provides the subject for one essay in *The Vagrant Mood* (he compares stories of pure detection with those

of the so-called hard-boiled school of Dashiell Hammett and Raymond Chandler) and, in *Points of View*, the short story provides another ("I like best the sort of story I can write myself. This is the sort of story that many people have written well, but no one more brilliantly than Maupassant"). On the whole, however, Maugham, even in these essays, approaches literature from the standpoint of the maker of it, defining genres in terms of their practitioners, those who, in his opinion, have worked best in the particular form.

Perhaps the most revealing group of works of all that Maugham wrote in this category are the prefaces to his own work, collected separately in *Selected Prefaces and Introductions of W. Somerset Maugham* (1963). Here the prefatory material written for the collected stories and plays is joined with other material written to precede collections of work by other authors, including the lengthy group of selections known as the *Traveller's Library* edited by Maugham in the early thirties. In his selections for that volume, as well as in the later *Tellers of Tales*, Maugham shows the same preoccupation with craft and the simple style that dominates his own work and that is enunciated so clearly in his prefaces. In the first of these collections the novels and short stories are chosen especially for their strong stories and immediate appeal. So, too, are most of the novels for which Maugham wrote prefaces in the volume *The Art of Fiction* (1955).

Maugham left no major work in the genre of literary criticism, but his minor productions, written mostly as occasional pieces, have a consistency that makes them useful and pleasurable reading for anyone concerned with the total accomplishment of their author. Whereas one can infer from the fiction and drama of Maugham the principles discussed in these works, they provide an outright statement of values by the author, who saw himself as a man of letters.

Travel essays comprise the third major category of work by Maugham that is neither fiction nor drama, and of the

books in this group certainly the most interesting and the best
is *Don Fernando*. I have already remarked on its success from
the standpoint of style. All of the excesses of the earlier book
on Spain, *The Land of the Blessed Virgin*, have been exor-
cised; it presents its subject plainly, in the author's voice, and
in the first person. Its chief fault lies in its loose organization,
yet it conveys a strong sense of the Spain that attracted
Maugham from early in his life and remained fascinating to
him to the end.

Most interesting and revealing of all the sections of the
book is the one devoted to El Greco. In *Of Human Bondage*,
Maugham had described Philip's fascination with the passion implicit in El Greco's work; in *Don Fernando* the older
Maugham becomes more specific, speculating that El Greco
was a homosexual. Remarking that artists' sexual lives seldom have much bearing on their work, he goes on to suggest
that in El Greco's case that might not be true. Writing from
the standpoint of a heterosexual who does not quite approve
of it all, Maugham suggests that El Greco's work combines in
varying degrees qualities of "flippancy," "sardonic humour,"
"wilfulness," a decorative sense of beauty, "elegance," fantasy,
and theatricalism, all of which he sees as characteristic of the
homosexual. While this view of El Greco's work has some
interest in itself, it is far more interesting for what it says
about Maugham. Here is one of the few times in his work
that Maugham refers directly to one of the most important
aspects of his own life. (The other major instance comes in a
discussion of Melville in *The Art of Fiction*.) In this context it
is worth noting that Maugham distances himself from the
subject as much as possible. It is also worth noting that he
links El Greco's homosexuality to his Mediterranean background, as though the years the artist spent in Crete and then
in Italy somehow explain his sexual inclination.

Apart from the section on El Greco, *Don Fernando* is
still worth reading for its evocation of the atmosphere of

Spain. In this it shares a quality with all of Maugham's work in this category: a strong sense of place and the ability to bring it to life for the reader. In his short stories, with a few sentences, Maugham often manages the same thing. In the travel books—which also include *On a Chinese Screen* (1922) and *The Gentleman in the Parlour* (1930)—he is more expansive in his descriptions, but no less evocative of the places he has seen.

8

~~~~~~

The Summing Up

Longevity, the narrator of *Cakes and Ale* observes, is for the writer its own reward. It certainly was for Maugham as he grew older. In the 1930s and 1940s his books were instant best-sellers and their author was increasingly revered as a great man of letters. In the 1950s, as Maugham entered the final decade of his life, the great man of letters become the grand old man; like the somewhat younger Noel Coward in the following decade, Maugham had the experience of becoming an institution in his own lifetime. For practically the first time in his literary career, the richness of his reputation approached the richness of his purse; Maugham's literary achievement, as he neared the end of his life, seemed larger than ever before.[1]

For many critics, however, it was a case of the life being long and the art a trifle short. Edmund Wilson, in his well-known essay in *The New Yorker*, led the attack, but the charges were familiar and always basically the same.[2] To his detractors, Maugham was always a second-rater who wrote with his eye on the charts. He accommodated public taste in various ways, thereby earning a fortune but sacrificing the right to be taken seriously as a writer. To this view, even his best work was marred by its tendency to sentimentalize or to reach pat conclusions about human behavior. As a stylist, though generally economical, he tended toward the predictable phrase. As a critic of letters he could not be taken seriously at all. As a human being, as seen in his own work, he was a bundle of biases, mean in spirit and limited in range.

Others took a different view. To these critics, scholars, and fellow-writers (including Evelyn Waugh), Maugham was at least a fine craftsman—in Waugh's words "the only living studio-master under whom one can study with profit"—and, to some, a genuine example of a disappearing type, the man of letters. Too many of Maugham's admirers, however, begin on a defensive note. They spend their time justifying serious consideration of his work rather than explaining what it is that makes his best work good. With few exceptions, no truly balanced, extended view of Maugham's work appeared until Ted Morgan's biography, which, while not a work of criticism, is nevertheless acute in its comments on Maugham's achievements.[3] Perhaps to some extent a more balanced view has had to wait for the public revelation of Maugham's personal life. At the very least, Morgan's story suggests that Maugham's homosexuality is often close to the surface of his work, however much Maugham may have tried to avoid mention of it. Had Maugham felt differently about his homosexuality, or had he lived in a time in which public revelation of homosexuality was not regarded as some form of offense, would his work have been different? The emotional detachment and coolness of tone deliberately cultivated in his writing surely, in some way, are related to the conditions of his personal situation. In the same sense, the cynicism that Maugham personally felt about human motives is reflected in all he wrote. Does this attitude not also have its roots in the feelings of the lonely stammerer, cut off from others by his disability, always seeing in their activities a selfish motive? An author's work is generally of a piece with his life, and the connections between the two are sometimes more obvious than they may seem at first consideration. The merit of Morgan's biography is that it helps the reader to see connections important to a reading of Maugham's texts.

Of equal importance in a final evaluation of Maugham's achievement is the fact that he was to a large extent a commercial writer. As with other writers who approach their work first as a profession and only secondly as an art, one finds much in Maugham's work that simply does not deserve to be read any longer, or that, for one reason or another, has dated so badly that it can no longer be taken seriously. Some of the short fiction falls into this category, as do many of the plays and novels. Who now reads *The Hour Before the Dawn* or *Then and Now?* Who performs *Caesar's Wife* or *East of Suez?* Works long neglected sometimes surprise in reprint or revival, but clearly the work of Maugham that will continue to prove worth reading is for the most part what has been looked at in this study.

Even in the best work, however, there are qualities that are troubling and that will never be accepted by some as characteristic of first-rate literature. Maugham's attitude toward women provides an obvious example. Were Maugham alive today, writing in the manner he frequently does about the relationships of men and women, some of his stories would not achieve print. Few readers today can accept such chauvinism uncritically, and women in his work too often fall into the categories of love goddess or bitch.

Another quality of Maugham's work that is unsatisfying is his frequent prejudice against Jews. In his work they are too frequently treated according to familiar stereotypes, in spite of the fact that Maugham maintained a number of lifetime friendships with Jews. The Nazis found the short story "The Alien Corn" worth citing because of its suggestion that Jews are always foreigners, regardless of the country in which they live.[4] (Although the narrator—the usual Maugham persona— feels much sympathy with the young man who is central to the story, he also manages to describe his Uncle Ferdy in distinctly stereotypical terms.) In Maugham's work, the same attitude sometimes reveals itself in references to Orientals and other colonial types, as well as to members of the lower classes.

Perhaps even worse from an artistic standpoint is the general falsification of experience encountered too often in his pages. Some of this falsification comes from the desire to shape the story to a particular end—to give the final paragraph or line some punch. Some derives from the simple failure, from whatever cause, to present outcomes in a believable way: the romantic ending of *Of Human Bondage*, the rather flat final chapters of *Cakes and Ale*, the passages in *The Razor's Edge* in which Maugham discusses Isabel's life—these portions of Maugham's work, all of which begin with situations that command attention, leave one with the feeling of having been slightly cheated, with the disappointment that comes inevitably when a work of fiction fails to satisfy. If some authors tend to open up the end of their story, suggesting too many possibilities for their characters, Maugham tends toward the opposite extreme, closing down the aperture till only a single object remains in view. This procedure is quite consistent with Maugham's idea that all art should have a definite end and that all human behavior is in the end predictable, but it is not always artistically satisfying.

Every criticism of Maugham's work, however, can be turned to praise. Though often condescending, he can treat members of the lower classes with great sympathy, as the early novel *Liza of Lambeth* and certain parts of *Of Human Bondage* show. In his indulgence in racial stereotyping, he is also not alone among modern authors. Even Joyce—whose treatment of a character of Jewish descent in the person of Leopold Bloom is remarkable for its sympathy and insight—is capable of indulging in the worst sort of stereotyping when he creates a vaudeville version of a black male in *Ulysses*.[5] Prejudice is never justified by the frequency of its occurrence, but Maugham is not in any sense unique among modern authors in occasionally showing it. Nor is he unique—as modern readers are acutely aware—in his stereotyping of women.

Maugham is also not the only author of his generation to produce markedly commercial work. In this regard the examples of Graham Greene and Evelyn Waugh come instantly to mind. Among Waugh's novels and Greene's there are numerous works whose purpose is primarily commercial, and Greene has been particularly fortunate in writing novels that were later made into successful screenplays, sometimes with himself as the scenarist. The modern authors who have had the luxury of writing without commercial or financial considerations frequently determining what they do are few and far between. Although one might say that in Maugham's case these considerations loomed especially large, one cannot say that he was unique in having them.

The emotional distance characteristic of Maugham gives rise, in his best work, to an ironic and sometimes witty view of human experiences. The very detachment of the narrator's view makes the characters and events in such works as *Cakes and Ale* or *The Razor's Edge* stand out in a special way. It is often minor characters, like Alroy Kear or Elliott Templeton, who emerge most strongly in this process, but in all of Maugham's fiction there are memorable scenes that reflect the dramatist's eye and attest to the validity of Maugham's narrative approach.

This approach to narrative depends upon a particular manner of telling, which insinuates the attention, capturing it much as a good story told after dinner holds one to its end. When exercised properly, this is a notable talent indeed, and Maugham usually shows that he knows just how far to carry it. He seldom writes about anything not within his range, nor does he force his material to suit the requirements of his approach. Some of the early novels, written before that approach was developed, show what could happen when such judgment was not being exercised. What ultimately satisfies the reader most in the best of Maugham's work is its strong sense of form — a sense of form that manifests itself especially well in the short stories, the shorter novels, and the plays — and its consistent tone.

In the end, however, one must conclude that the greatest single achievement in Maugham's oeuvre does not qualify very well on any of these counts. It is not tightly conceived, though it has some very fine scenes; it is not written in the carefully cultivated style of the later fiction; it also notably lacks an ironic tone, although the writer shows considerable distance from his main character — himself. I refer of course to *Of Human Bondage*, which remains, all things considered, Maugham's greatest accomplishment.

Notes

1. Disorder and Early Sorrow: Maugham's Life and Times

1. The definitive biography is Ted Morgan's *Maugham* (New York: Simon and Schuster, 1980). Anyone interested in Maugham will find this work essential; it supersedes all previous biographies. Some readers complain of its coldness toward its subject, but that perhaps is a reflection of Maugham's personality, not Morgan's; at any rate it is an honest view of Maugham's life and work, not an apologia. I am indebted to Morgan's account of the life, as well as to his interpretation of individual works.

2. This is not the place for a catalog, but the number of contemporary English authors for whom the homosexual experience was in some way significant is amazingly long and includes such diverse talents as E. M. Forster, Noel Coward, and Evelyn Waugh. Forster's work reflects the experience more than anyone else's, but the work reflecting his homosexuality remained largely unknown in his lifetime.

3. See especially Morgan's reading of the early novel, *Mrs. Craddock*, pp. 91–92.

4. It had two performances in its initial production, but it was revived the following year for a run of twenty-eight performances. For these statistics, see Raymond Mander and Joe Mitchenson, *Theatrical Companion to Maugham* (London: Rockliff, 1955).

2. Troubled Grace: *Of Human Bondage*

1. The turning point in the novel's critical reception, which was initially somewhat cool, came with the review by Theodore

Dreiser, "As a Realist Sees It," in *The New Republic* 5 (December 25, 1915), pp. 202–4.

2. Morgan, pp. 196–97.

3. This is not to say, of course, that all homosexual relationships are one-sided, sadomasochistic, or chaste. It is appropriate, given the artistic background that is so prominent in the book, that Mildred should be represented in an androgynous fashion. Art of the late nineteenth and early twentieth centuries abounds in androgynous figures. The work of the English Pre-Raphaelites is especially rich in this respect, and so is the work of Oscar Wilde's friend Aubrey Beardsley. Representative types from the period are to be found in Philippe Roberts-Jones, *Beyond Time and Place: Non-Realist Painting in the Nineteenth Century* (Oxford: Oxford University Press, 1978), and Philippe Jullian, *The Symbolists* (London: Phaidon, 1973).

4. Maurice Beebe's *Ivory Towers and Sacred Founts: The Artist as Hero in Fiction from Goethe to Joyce* (New York: New York University Press, 1964) presents an overview of the subject. The term *Erziehungsroman* may also be applied to *Of Human Bondage*.

5. In chapter 81: "He found the work of absorbing interest. There was humanity there in the rough, the materials the artist worked on; and Philip felt a curious thrill when it occurred to him that he was in the position of the artist and the patients were like clay in his hands."

6. On the treatment of artists and painting in the novel, see Stanley Archer, "Artists and Paintings in Maugham's *Of Human Bondage*," *English Literature in Transition* 14 (1971), pp. 181–89. For a view of Maugham's personal taste in painting, see *Catalogue of The Collection of Impressionist and Modern Pictures Formed by W. Somerset Maugham over the Last Fifty Years*, catalog of auction at Sotheby and Co., London, April 10, 1962; see also Raymond Mander and Joe Mitchenson, *The Artist and the Theatre: The Story of the Paintings Collected and Presented to the National Theatre by W. Somerset Maugham*, with an introduction by Maugham (London: Heinemann, 1955).

7. Samuel Butler reaches much the same conclusion, though with different imagery, in *The Way of All Flesh*:

> Accidents which happen to a man before he is born, in the persons of his ancestors, will, if he remembers them at all, leave an indelible impression on him; they will have moulded his character so that, do what he will, it is hardly possible for him to escape their consequences. If a man is to enter into the Kingdom of Heaven, he must do so, not only as a little child, but as a little embryo, or rather as a little zoosperm — and not only this, but as one that has come of zoosperms which have entered into the Kingdom of Heaven before him for many generations. Accidents which occur for the first time, and belong to the period since a man's last birth, are not, as a general rule, so permanent in their effects, though of course they may sometimes be so.

Butler's universe, like the one depicted in *Of Human Bondage*, is essentially deterministic. See the discussion of the passage by Morton Dauwen Zabel in the Modern Library edition of 1950, p. xix.

3. Instruction and Delight:
The Moon
and Sixpence and *Cakes and Ale*

1. Wilmon Menard's "Somerset Maugham and Paul Gauguin," *Michigan Quarterly Review* 7 (1968), pp. 227–32, pursues these connections. See also the general studies of Maugham's work listed in the bibliography at the end of this volume; the relationship between Charles Strickland and Gauguin is treated, at least briefly, in most of these works. In general, as with his use of the life of Hardy in *Cakes and Ale*, Maugham took liberties with the life of Gauguin, making no effort to follow it precisely in developing Strickland's character.
2. Morgan deals with the biographical element in *Cakes and Ale* in detail, pp. 334–42. R. Barton Palmer's "Artists and Hacks: Maugham's *Cakes and Ale*," *South Atlantic Review* 46

(1981), pp. 54–63, discusses generally the treatment of writers in the novel.

3.   Even more so than with a painter like Henri ("*le Douanier*")
     Rousseau, Gauguin's primitivism is highly refined and subjec-
     tive; he uses primitive art both as model and as inspiration,
     but he makes it totally his own. On this subject, see Wayne
     Andersen, *Gauguin's Paradise Lost* (New York: Viking Press,
     1971).

4.   See the posthumous collection *Seventeen Lost Stories by W.
     Somerset Maugham*, compiled and introduced by Craig V.
     Showalter (Garden City: Doubleday, 1969). The first six sto-
     ries in this collection are those originally published under the
     title *Orientations* and never republished in Maugham's life-
     time. The very first of these, "The Punctiliousness of Don
     Sebastian," which dates from 1898, was Maugham's first pub-
     lished short story and is in the first person. In its narrative
     strategy, with the main action of the story framed by the first-
     person narration, this story is very much like those from later
     in Maugham's career. Butler's *The Way of All Flesh* did not
     see the light of day until 1903, a year after its author's death.
     It was clearly an influence on *Of Human Bondage*, but not on
     the earliest fiction by Maugham.

5.   Morgan describes the problem in the following way: "Unless
     it results from a physical defect, which in Maugham's case it
     apparently did not, a stammer would appear to be self-inflict-
     ed. The stammerer has some quarrel with himself, he sets up
     his own roadblocks. Stammering becomes a self-fulfilling
     prophesy. The stammerer knows he will be made fun of, and
     he is. Stammering is a way of guaranteeing the situation that
     you foresee." (p. 16)

4. Innocents Abroad: *The Razor's Edge*

1.   Maugham novelized an early play that attempted the same
     thing and called it *The Merry-go-round*. He writes of it in
     The Summing Up:

I took a larger number of persons than I had ever sought to cope with before and devised four or five independent stories. They were attached to one another by a very thin thread, an elderly woman who knew at least one person in each group. The book was called *The Merry-go-round*. It was rather absurd because owing to the influence on me of the aesthetic school of the nineties I made everyone incredibly beautiful, and it was written in a tight and affected manner. But its chief defect was that it lacked the continuous line that directs the reader's interest; the stories were not after all of equal importance and it was tiresome to divert one's attention from one set of people to another. I failed from my ignorance of the very simple device of seeing the diverse events and the characters that took part in them through the eyes of a single person. It is a device which of course the autobiographical novel has used for centuries, but which Henry James has very usefully developed. By the simple process of writing *he* for *I* and stepping down from the omniscience of an all-knowing narrator to the imperfect acquaintance of a participator he showed how to give unity and verisimilitude to a story.

2. See Morgan, p. 480.

3. Maugham, according to Morgan (p. 481), to some extent had in mind a specific person when he created the character of Elliott: Henry (Chips) Channon, who, like Elliott, was a wealthy American who much admired the English aristocracy.

4. L. Brander, in *Somerset Maugham: A Guide* (New York: Barnes & Noble, 1963; reprint 1965), also notes this resemblance, p. 109. *The Road Uphill*, an unproduced play of 1924, is even closer to *The Razor's Edge*. See the synopsis in Mander and Mitchenson, *Theatrical Companion*, pp. 195–99.

5. The Bradley living room, which combines art and furniture of different periods and schools, "was hideous and yet, I don't know why, agreeable. It had a homely, lived-in air and you felt that the incredible jumble had a significance." In *The Razor's Edge*, it is Elliott Templeton who has the good taste.

6. "This attitude may be regarded as an integral and controlling part of his personality as revealed in his writings. It is not so much cynicism as clinicism; a dispassionate and systematic habit of observation more often found among descriptive sci-

entists than among creative artists." John Brophy, *Somerset Maugham*, no. 22 of *Writers and Their Work* (London: Longmans, Green [for the British Council and the National Book League], rev. ed., 1958), p. 11. Brophy goes on to compare Maugham's attitude with that of Maupassant, disciple of Gustave Flaubert (whose father was a physician). Frederic Raphael pursues some relationships between Maugham's medical training and his fiction in "Fiction and the Medical Mode," *Journal of the Eighteen Nineties Society* 6-7 (1975-76), pp. 5-12.

7. "The Art of Fiction," from the book of the same title (Garden City, NY: Doubleday, 1955), pp. 23-24.

8. Brophy, p. 28.

9. The more recent of the versions of *The Razor's Edge* is the one by Bill Murray released in 1984. While this film has many virtues as an adaptation of the novel and some excellent performances in contrast with the earlier version, it does not include the character of Maugham, thus removing the key feature of the narrative. Robert L. Calder, in "Somerset Maugham and the Cinema," *Literature/Film Quarterly* 6 (1978), pp. 262-73, surveys film adaptations of Maugham's work, including the first version of *The Razor's Edge*.

5. White Mischief: Maugham's Short Fiction

1. An exception is *East of Suez*, a melodrama written and produced in 1922.

2. "Sinclair Lewis," in *Abinger Harvest* (New York: Meridian Books, 1955), p. 123.

3. It is in fact possible, especially in the early pages of this story, to substitute first-person for third-person references to Doctor MacPhail and in no way do any disservice to our sense of the story or to MacPhail's part in it. Here, for instance, is the opening passage, with the changes indicated in italics:

It was nearly bed-time and when *we* awoke next morning land would be in sight. *I* lit *my* pipe and, leaning over the rail, searched the

> heavens for the Southern Cross. After two years at the front and a wound that had taken longer to heal than it should, *I* was glad to settle down quietly at Apia for twelve months at least, and *I* felt already better for the journey.

This is in many respects a typical opening to a first-person Maugham story.

4. See for example Poe's review of "Hawthorne's *Tales*," reprinted in *The Shock of Recognition: The Development of Literature in the United States Recorded by the Men Who Made It* (New York: Farrar, Straus and Cudahy, 1955), edited by Edmund Wilson, especially pp. 162–65. From such reviews Poe's principles of fiction are to be inferred. The development of the short story, as Poe was well aware, was linked to the development of the large-circulation magazines that published them.

5. Morgan, pp. 252–53. In "Changing Views of Empire: The Imperial Themes of Somerset Maugham," *Research Studies* (Washington State University), 47 (September 1979), pp. 145–53, Kathryne S. McDorman deals generally with the treatment of the British empire in Maugham's work, comparing the prewar and postwar views.

6. Preface to *The Complete Short Stories*, vol. 1 (*East and West*) (Garden City, NY: Doubleday, 1934), p. vii.

7. "The Short Story," in *Points of View* (London: Heinemann, 1958), p. 155.

8. Maugham saw the device of the first-person narrator limiting his range in storytelling: "It makes it possible for the writer to tell no more than he knows. Making no claim to omniscience, he can frankly say when a motive or an occurrence is unknown to him, and thus often give his story a plausibility that it might otherwise lack. It tends also to put the reader on intimate terms with the author" (preface to *Complete Short Stories*, vol. 1, p. xv). This last comment leads to the observation of John Brophy: "He is less a writer than a talker — a view of him which is supported by the character of his prose and the construction of his novels and stories, and which is consonant with his success in the necessarily oral conventions of the

theatre and cinema" (*Somerset Maugham*, p. 25). The second-person paragraph in "Rain" is the one beginning "Iwelei was on the edge of the city."

9.   As in the work of the Italian futurists, which preceded the First World War by five years or more. For the theoretical basis for such polygeneric work, later of significance to the surrealists, see F. T. Marinetti, *Selected Writings* (New York: Farrar, Straus and Giroux, 1972). Needless to say, such experimentalism was anathema to Maugham.

10. For background on Maugham in Russia, see Rhodri Jeffreys-Jones, "W. Somerset Maugham: Anglo-American Agent in Revolutionary Russia," *American Quarterly* 28 (1979), pp. 90–106. Morgan also provides an account, pp. 226–32.

11. Indeed, Maugham, with the character of Ashenden the spy, may be said to have begun a tradition that remains very much alive. It is much as if Dr. Watson, not Sherlock Holmes, were the main character in the stories by Arthur Conan Doyle. But Ashenden is in no sense a bungler or a fool; it is his job that is unexceptional, not himself.

12. Introduction to *Cakes and Ale and Twelve Short Stories*, selected by Angus Wilson (Garden City, NY: Doubleday, 1967), p. 7.

6. Wit's End: Maugham's Work for the Theater

1.   Of all the plays, *The Circle* and *The Constant Wife*, both of which are representative of Maugham and of their types, show the best signs of permanent life. *Our Betters* also has much life. There are surprises, too; a recent television revival showed *Sheppey*, Maugham's last play, to have much more to it than one might suppose from a mere reading of the text.

2.   Ronald E. Barnes, in *The Dramatic Comedy of William Somerset Maugham* (The Hague: Mouton, 1968), surveys the comedies from early to late, comparing their treatment of marriage and other themes.

3.   *The Circle* stretches the form as far as it can be stretched, however. See the discussion of antitheses important to the play

in Martin Jackey, "*The Circle* de S. Maugham: Critique des illusions et illusions de la critique," *Cahiers Victoriens et Edouardiens: Revue du Centre d'Etudes et de Recherches Victoriennes* 9–10 (1979), pp. 203–17.

4. These terms are conveniences that become less convenient when pursued with the example of specific plays, but if we take Wilde as a model of one form and Feydeau as a model of the other, we can see the difference easily.

7. The Lion of the Villa Mauresque: The Essays and Memoirs

1. In *The Moon and Sixpence* Maugham paid tribute to the artist as rebel against society. By the time he wrote *Cakes and Ale* he had modified that view somewhat, showing Edward Driffield's success to be a result of accommodation as much as rebellion. In *The Summing Up* he virtually rejects the notion of rebellion altogether. If the artist is free, his freedom is a private matter, implying no antisocial position.

2. On this matter, see Morgan, p. 343.

8. The Summing Up

1. In 1950, at the very beginning of the last productive decade for Maugham, author and editor Whit Burnett produced an anthology of work by the best living authors. His list was derived from a survey of authors, editors, journalists, critics, reviewers, educators, librarians, miscellaneous public figures, bookstore personnel, and general readers. Maugham figured most prominently in the lists from authors, editors, reviewers, United States PEN Club members, bookstore personnel, and miscellaneous public figures; overall, he was twelfth in a list of the fifty most voted upon, with 427 votes from all sources. By comparison, Shaw, who came first in the list, had 539 votes. Only one other English author, Aldous Huxley, had more votes, coming in ninth place with 434. (T. S. Eliot, also

counted by Burnett as English, was eighth, with 435 votes.)
One survey, done with a selective population, for one antholo-
gy, proves little, but the people surveyed by Burnett make an
impressive list, and the results are fairly indicative of
Maugham's standing in the literary world in 1950. *The
World's Best*, ed. Whit Burnett (New York: Dial, 1950).

2. Wilson's essay, collected under the title "The Apotheosis of
    Somerset Maugham" in *Classics and Commercials* (New
    York: Farrar, Straus, 1950), pp. 319–26, is essentially a re-
    view of the novel *Then and Now*, but, from the beginning, it
    takes a negative view of Maugham's entire achievement.
    Wilson's viewpoint—which sees Maugham's work as second-
    rate at best—is typical of that of the detractors.

3. The principal scholarly studies not already mentioned are
    Richard A. Cordell, *Somerset Maugham: A Biographical and
    Critical Study* (Bloomington: Indiana University Press, 1961);
    M. K. Naik, *W. Somerset Maugham* (Norman: University of
    Oklahoma, 1966); Robert Lorin Calder, *W. Somerset
    Maugham and the Quest for Freedom* (Garden City, NY:
    Doubleday, 1973); and Anthony Curtis, *The Pattern of
    Maugham: A Critical Portrait* (New York: Taplinger, 1974).
    The first two of these are somewhat weak critically; all four
    depend upon a biographical-critical approach to their subject,
    which, in Calder and in Curtis, frequently yields valuable
    insights. Evelyn Waugh's comment on Maugham comes from
    his review of the novel *Christmas Holiday*, in *The Essays,
    Articles and Reviews of Evelyn Waugh*, ed. Donat Gallagher
    (Boston: Little, Brown, 1984), pp. 247–48. Forrest D. Burt's
    recently published *W. Somerset Maugham* (Boston: Twayne
    Publishers, 1985) says little new on the subject.

4. Morgan, p. 141. *Lady Frederick*, the play of 1907, contains a
    Jewish caricature in the person of Captain Montgomerie.

5. In the celebrated Night-Town episode, where fantasy and real-
    ity intermingle. The Jewish prejudice occurs in the work of
    other major figures such as T. S. Eliot and Ezra Pound.

Bibliography

I. Principal Works by W. Somerset Maugham (arranged chronologically by date of publication of the first edition; individual plays arranged by date of writing and first production)

A. NOVELS

Liza of Lambeth, London: T. Fisher Unwin, 1897.
The Making of a Saint. Boston: L. C. Page, 1898.
The Hero. London: Hutchinson and Co., 1901.
Mrs. Craddock. London: William Heinemann, 1902.
The Merry-go-round. London: William Heinemann, 1904.
Of Human Bondage. New York: George H. Doran, 1915.
The Moon and Sixpence. London: William Heinemann, 1919.
The Painted Veil. New York: George H. Doran, 1925.
Cakes and Ale. London: William Heinemann Ltd., 1930.
The Narrow Corner. London: William Heinemann Ltd., 1932.
Theatre. Garden City, NY: Doubleday, Doran and Company, 1937.
Christmas Holiday. London: William Heinemann Ltd., 1939.
Up at the Villa. New York: Doubleday, Doran and Company, 1941
The Hour Before the Dawn. Garden City, NY: Doubleday, Doran and Company, 1942.
The Razor's Edge. Garden City, NY: Doubleday, Doran and Company, 1944.
Then and Now. London: William Heinemann Ltd., 1946.
Catalina. London: William Heinemann Ltd., 1948.

B. SHORT FICTION

Orientations. London: T. Fisher Unwin, 1899.
The Trembling of a Leaf. New York: George H. Doran, 1921.
The Casuarina Tree. London: William Heinemann Ltd., 1926.

Ashenden: Or The British Agent. London: William Heinemann Ltd., 1928.
Six Stories Written in the First Person Singular. Garden City, NY: Doubleday, Doran and Company, 1931.
Ah King. London: William Heinemann Ltd., 1933.
Cosmopolitans. Garden City, NY: Doubleday, Doran and Company, 1936.
The Mixture as Before. London: William Heinemann Ltd., 1940.
Creatures of Circumstance. London: William Heinemann Ltd., 1947.
The Complete Short Stories of W. Somerset Maugham. 3 vols. London: William Heinemann Ltd., 1951.
The Complete Short Stories of W. Somerset Maugham. 2 vols. Garden City, NY: Doubleday and Company, 1952.

C. NONFICTION

The Land of the Blessed Virgin. London: William Heinemann, 1905.
On a Chinese Screen. New York: George H. Doran, 1922.
The Gentleman in the Parlour. London: William Heinemann Ltd., 1930.
Don Fernando. London: William Heinemann Ltd., 1935.
The Summing Up. London: William Heinemann Ltd., 1938.
Strictly Personal. Garden City, NY: Doubleday, Doran and Company, 1941.
A Writer's Notebook. London: William Heinemann Ltd., 1949.
The Writer's Point of View. London: Published for the National Book League by the Cambridge University Press, 1951.
The Vagrant Mood. London: William Heinemann Ltd., 1952.
Ten Novels and Their Authors. London: William Heinemann Ltd., 1954. [American title: *The Art of Fiction.*]
Points of View. London: William Heinemann Ltd., 1958.
Purely for My Pleasure. London: William Heinemann Ltd., 1962.
Selected Prefaces and Introductions of W. Somerset Maugham. Garden City, NY: Doubleday and Company, 1963.

D. DRAMA

A Man of Honour (written 1898; revised 1902; produced 1903).
Lady Frederick (1903; produced 1907).
Mrs. Dot (1904; 1908).
Jack Straw (1905; 1908).
Penelope (1908; 1909).
Smith (1909).
The Tenth Man (1909; 1910).
Grace (1910).
The Land of Promise (1913).
Our Betters (1915; 1917).
Caroline (*The Unattainable*) (1915; 1916).
Love in a Cottage (1917; 1918).
Caesar's Wife (1918; 1919).
Too Many Husbands (British title *Home and Beauty*) (1919).
The Circle (1919; 1921).
The Unknown (1920).
East of Suez (1922).
The Camel's Back (1923).
The Constant Wife (1926).
The Letter (1926; 1927).
The Sacred Flame (1928).
The Breadwinner (1930).
For Services Rendered (1932).
Sheppey (1933).
The Collected Plays of W. Somerset Maugham. 3 vols. London:
    William Heinemann Ltd., 1952.

E. POSTHUMOUS WORKS

Maugham, W. Somerset. *A Traveller in Romance: Uncollected
    Writings, 1901–1964*. Ed. John Whitehead. New York:
    Clarkson N. Potter, 1984.
Seventeen Lost Stories by W. Somerset Maugham. Compiled and
    with introduction by Craig V. Showalter. Garden City, NY:
    Doubleday and Company, 1969.

II. Principal Works about W. Somerset Maugham (The following list is highly selective and does not include articles and other short pieces; for these see the notes to individual chapters or the bibliographies listed below.)

A. BIBLIOGRAPHIES OF WORKS BY OR ABOUT MAUGHAM (INCLUDING CATALOG OF ART COLLECTION)

Catalogue of The Collection of Impressionist and Modern Pictures Formed by W. Somerset Maugham over the Last Fifty Years. London: Sotheby and Co., 10 April 1962.

Mander, Raymond, and Joe Mitchenson. *Theatrical Companion to Maugham: A Pictorial Record of the First Performances of the Plays of W. Somerset Maugham.* With an appreciation by J. C. Trewin. London: Rockliff, 1955.

Stott, Raymond Toole. *A Bibliography of the Works of W. Somerset Maugham.* Rev. and extended ed. London: Kaye and Ward, 1973.

W. Somerset Maugham: An Annotated Bibliography of Writings about Him. Compiled and ed. by Charles Sanders. DeKalb, IL: Northern Illinois University Press, 1970.

B. BIOGRAPHIES, CRITICAL WORKS, AND MONOGRAPHS

Barnes, Ronald E. *The Dramatic Comedy of William Somerset Maugham.* The Hague: Mouton, 1968.

Brander, L[aurence]. *Somerset Maugham: A Guide.* New York: Barnes and Noble, 1963; reprint 1965.

Brophy, John. *Writers and Their Work.* No. 22, *Somerset Maugham.* Rev. ed. London: Published for the British Council and the National Book League by Longmans, Green, 1958.

Brown, Ivor. *W. Somerset Maugham.* London: International Textbook Co., 1970.

Burt, Forrest D. *W. Somerset Maugham.* Twayne's English Authors Series. Boston: Twayne Publishers, 1985.

Calder, Robert Lorin. *W. Somerset Maugham and the Quest for Freedom.* Garden City, NY: Doubleday and Company, 1973.

Cordell, Richard A. *Somerset Maugham: A Biographical and Critical Study*. Rev. ed. Bloomington: Indiana University Press, 1969.

Curtis, Anthony. *The Pattern of Maugham: A Critical Portrait*. New York: Taplinger, 1974.

_____. *Somerset Maugham*. Windsor, Berkshire, England: Profile Books, 1982.

Mander, Raymond, and Joe Mitchenson. *The Artist and the Theatre: The Story of the Paintings Collected and Presented to the National Theatre by W. Somerset Maugham*. Introduction by Maugham. London: William Heinemann Ltd., 1955.

Maugham, W. Somerset. *The Maugham Enigma: An Anthology*. Ed. Klaus W. Jonas. London: P. Owen; New York: Citadel, 1954.

_____.*The World of Somerset Maugham*. Ed. Klaus W. Jonas. Westport, CT: Greenwood Press, 1959.

Morgan, Ted. *Maugham*. New York: Simon and Schuster, 1980.

Naik, M. K. *W. Somerset Maugham*. Norman: University of Oklahoma, 1966.

Waugh, Evelyn. *The Essays, Articles and Reviews of Evelyn Waugh*. Ed. Donat Gallagher. Boston: Little, Brown, 1984.

Index

Alanson, Bert, 10
"Alien Corn, The," 112
Androcles and the Lion (Shaw), 95
Aristotle, 99
Arrowsmith (Lewis), 63
Art, qualities of, 101
Art of Fiction, The, 107, 108
Ashenden, 9, 69, 79–81, 104
Audience, for theater, 83–84
Augustan period, 102
Autobiographical novel, 8, 14, 29, 36, 56

Babbitt (Lewis), 63
Bates, H. E., 79
Beauty, 101
  in painting, 21
Bildungsroman tradition, 32–34
Blake, William, 43
Boccaccio, Giovanni, 69
Breadwinner, The, 92, 93
Brecht, Bertolt, 84
British drama, *see* English drama
Brooks, Ellingham, 5, 30
Brophy, John, 68, 69
Burke, Edmund, 106
Butler, Samuel, 32, 55, 56

Caesar's Wife, 85, 112
Cakes and Ale, 8, 11, 39, 47–57, 58, 65, 69, 80, 110, 113, 114
  characters in, 60
  as comic novel, 37–38, 47
  end of, 49–50, 57
  first-person narration in, 55–56
  initiation in, 52–54
  irony in, 55
  plot of, 47–50
  structure of, 57
  two novels in, 54, 57
Caroline, 85
Cavalcade (Coward), 93, 94
Cervantes, Miguel de, 69
Chamberlain, Neville, 102
Chandler, Raymond, 107
Chekhov, Anton, 60, 77, 84
Cherry Orchard, The (Chekhov), 60
Chronicle novel, 60
Churchill, Sir Winston, 102
Circle, The, 7, 10, 85–90, 91, 92, 96
  characters in, 89
  decision to run off in, 88–89
  dialogue in, 90
  plot of, 85–88
  title of, 85